D1017147

Anthology of Best-Loved Poems

See p. **151**

TO BEHOLD THE WANDERING MOON
RIDING NEAR HER HIGHEST NOON

Anthology of Best-Loved Poems

~

Edited by
ANDREW LANG

With Illustrations by H. J. Ford and Lancelot Speed

GRAMERCY BOOKS
NEW YORK

This 2001 edition is published by Gramercy Books™, an imprint of Random House Value
Publishing, Inc. 280 Park Avenue, New York, N.Y. 10017.

Gramercy Books™ and design are trademarks of Random House Value Publishing, Inc.

Random House
New York • Toronto • London • Sydney • Auckland
http://www.randomhouse.com/

Printed and bound in the United States of America

A CIP catalogue record for this book is available from the Library of Congress.

ISBN 0-517-16272-5

9 8 7 6 5 4 3 2 1

INTRODUCTION

THE purpose of this Collection is to put before children, and young people, poems which are good in themselves, and especially fitted to live, as Theocritus says, 'on the lips of the young.' The Editor has been guided to a great extent, in making his choice, by recollections of what particularly pleased himself in youth. As a rule, the beginner in poetry likes what is called 'objective' art—verse with a story in it, the more vigorous the story the better. The old ballads satisfy this taste, and the Editor would gladly have added more of them, but for two reasons. First, there are parents who would see harm, where children see none, in 'Tamlane' and 'Clerk Saunders.' Next, there was reason to dread that the volume might become entirely too Scottish. It is certainly a curious thing that, in Mr. Palgrave's *Golden Treasury*, where some seventy poets are represented, scarcely more than a tenth of the number were born north of Tweed. In this book, however, intended for lads and lassies, the poems by Campbell, by Sir Walter Scott, by Burns, by the Scottish song-writers, and the Scottish minstrels of the ballad, are in an unexpectedly large proportion to the poems by English authors. The Editor believes that this predominance of Northern verse is not due to any exorbitant local patriotism of his own. The singers of the North, for some reason or other, do excel in poems of action and of adventure, or to him they seem to excel. He is acquainted with no modern ballad by a Southern English-man, setting aside 'Christabel' and the 'Ancient Mariner—' poems hardly to be called ballads—which equals 'The Eve of

St. John.' For spirit-stirring martial strains few Englishmen since Drayton have been rivals of Campbell, of Scott, of Burns, of Hogg with his song of 'Donald McDonald.' Two names, indeed, might be mentioned here : the names of the late Sir Francis Doyle and of Lord Tennyson. But the scheme of this book excludes a choice from contemporary poets. It is not necessary to dwell on the reasons for this decision. But the Editor believes that some anthologist of the future will find in the poetry of living English authors, or of English authors recently dead, a very considerable garden of that kind of verse which is good both for young and old. To think for a moment of this abundance is to conceive more highly of Victorian poetry. There must still, after all, be youth and mettle in the nation which could produce 'The Ballad of the Revenge,' 'Lucknow,' 'The Red Thread of Honour,' 'The Loss of the Birkenhead,' 'The Forsaken Merman,' 'The Bringing of the Good News to Ghent,' 'The Pied Piper of Hamelin,' and many a song of Charles Kingsley's, not to mention here the work of still later authors. But we only glean the fields of men long dead.

For this reason, then—namely, because certain admirable contemporary poems, like 'Lucknow' and 'The Red Thread of Honour,' are unavoidably excluded—the poems of action, of war, of adventure, chance to be mainly from Scottish hands. Thus Campbell and Scott may seem to hold a pre-eminence which would not have been so marked had the works of living poets, or of poets recently dead, been available. Yet in any circumstances these authors must have occupied a great deal of the field : Campbell for the vigour which the unfriendly Leyden had to recognise ; Scott for that Homeric quality which, since Homer, no man has displayed in the same degree. Extracts from his long poems do not come within the scope of this selection. But, estimated even by his lyrics, Scott seems, to the Editor, to justify his right, now occasionally disdained, to rank among the great poets of his country. He has music, speed, and gaiety, as in 'The Hunting Song' or in 'Nora's Vow : '

> For all the gold, for all the gear,
> For all the lands both far and near
> That ever valour lost or won,
> I would not wed the Earlie's son!

Lines like these sing themselves naturally in a child's memory, while there is a woodland freshness and a daring note in

> O, Brignall banks are wild and fair,
> And Greta woods are green.

'Young Lochinvar' goes 'as dauntingly as wantonly' to his bridal, as the heir of Macpherson's Rant to his death, in a wonderful swing and gallop of verse; while still, out of dim years of childhood far away, one hears how all the bells are ringing in Dunfermline town for the wedding of Alice Brand. From childhood, too, one remembers the quietism of Lucy Ashton's song, and the monotone of the measure—

> Vacant heart and hand and eye,
> Easy live and quiet die.

The wisdom of it is as perceptible to a child as that other lesson of Scott's, which rings like a clarion:

> To all the sensual world proclaim
> One glorious hour of crowded life·
> Is worth an age without a name.

Then there are his martial pieces, as the 'Gathering Song of Donald Dhu' and 'The Cavalier,' and there is the inimitable simplicity and sadness of 'Proud Maisie,' like the dirge for Clearista by Meleager, but with a deeper tone, a stronger magic; and there is the song, which the Fates might sing in a Greek chorus, the song which Meg Merrilies sang,

> Twist ye, twine ye, even so!

These are but a few examples of Scott's variety, his spontaneity, his hardly conscious mastery of his art. Like Phemius of Ithaca, he might say 'none has taught me but myself, and the God has put into my heart all manner of lays'—all but the conscious and elaborate 'manner of lays,' which has now such power over some young critics that they talk of Scott's redeeming his bad verse by his good novels. The taste of childhood and of maturity is simpler and more pure.

In the development of a love of poetry it is probable that simple, natural, and adventurous poetry like Scott's comes first, and that it is followed later—followed but not superseded —by admiration of such reflective poetry as is plain and even obvious, like that of Longfellow, from whom a number of examples are given. But, to the Editor at least, it seems that a child who cares for poetry is hardly ever too young to delight in mere beauty of words, in the music of metre and rhyme, even when the meaning is perhaps still obscure and little considered. A child, one is convinced, would take great pleasure in Mr. Swinburne's choruses in ' Atalanta,' such as

> Before the beginning of years,

and in Shelley's ' Cloud ' and his ' Arethusa.' For this reason a number of pieces of Edgar Poe's are given, and we have not shrunk even from including the faulty ' Ulalume,' because of the mere sound of it, apart from the sense. The three most famous poems of Coleridge may be above a child's full comprehension, but they lead him into a world not realised, ' an unsubstantial fairy place,' bright in a morning mist, like our memories of childhood.

It is probably later, in most lives, that the mind wakens to delight in the less obvious magic of style, and the less ringing, the more intimate melody of poets like Keats and Lord Tennyson. The songs of Shakespeare, of course, are for all ages, and the needs of youth comparatively mature are met in Dryden's ' Ode on Alexander's Feast,' and in ' Lycidas ' and the ' Hymn for the Nativity.'

It does not appear to the Editor that poems about children, or especially intended for children, are those which a child likes best. A child's imaginative life is much spent in the unknown future, and in the romantic past. He is the contemporary of Leonidas, of Agincourt, of Bannockburn, of the

'45 ; he is living in an heroic age of his own, in a
Phæacia where the Gods walk visibly. The poems written
for and about children, like Blake's and some of Wordsworth's,
rather appeal to the old, whose own childhood is now to them
a distant fairy world, as the man's life is to the child. The
Editor can remember having been more mystified and puzzled by
'Lucy Gray' than by the 'Eve of St. John,' at a very early age.
He is convinced that Blake's 'Nurse's Song,' for example, which
brings back to him the long, the endless evenings of the Northern
summer, when one had to go to bed while the hills beyond
Ettrick were still clear in the silver light, speaks more inti-
mately to the grown man than to the little boy or girl. Hood's
'I remember, I remember,' in the same way, brings in the
burden of reflection on that which the child cannot possibly
reflect upon—namely, a childhood which is past. There is the
same tone in Mr. Stevenson's ' Child's Garden of Verse,' which
can hardly be read without tears—tears that do not come and
should not come to the eyes of childhood. For, beyond the
child and his actual experience of the world as the ballads and
poems of battle are, he can forecast the years, and anticipate
the passions. What he cannot anticipate is his own age,
himself, his pleasures and griefs, as the grown man sees them
in memory, and with a sympathy for the thing that he has
been, and can never be again. It is his excursions into the
untravelled world which the child enjoys, and this is what
makes Shakespeare so dear to him—Shakespeare who has
written so little on childhood. In *The Midsummer Night's
Dream* the child can lose himself in a world familiar to him,
in the fairy age, and can derive such pleasure from Puck, or
from Ariel, as his later taste can scarce recover in the same
measure. Falstaff is his playfellow, ' a child's Falstaff, an
innocent creature,' as Dickens says of Tom Jones in *David
Copperfield.*

A boy prefers the wild Prince and Poins to Barbara
Lewthwaite, the little girl who moralised to the lamb. We
make a mistake when we ' write down ' to children ; still more
do we err when we tell a child not to read this or that

because he cannot understand it. He understands far more than we give him credit for, but nothing that can harm him. The half-understanding of it, too, the sense of a margin beyond, as in a wood full of unknown glades, and birds, and flowers unfamiliar, is great part of a child's pleasure in reading. For this reason many poems are included here in which the Editor does not suppose that the readers will be able to pass an examination. For another reason a few pieces of no great excellence as poetry are included. Though they may appear full of obviousness to us, there is an age of dawning reflection to which they are not obvious. Longfellow, especially, seems to the Editor to be a kind of teacher to bring readers to the more reflective poetry of Wordsworth, while he has a sort of simple charm in which there is a foretaste of the charm of Tennyson and Keats. But everyone who attempts to make such a collection must inevitably be guided by his own recollections of childhood, of his childish likings, and the development of the love of poetry in himself. We have really no other criterion, for children are such kind and good-natured critics that they will take pleasure in whatever is given or read to them, and it is hard for us to discern where the pleasure is keenest and most natural.

The Editor trusts that this book may be a guide into romance and fairyland to many children. Of a child's enthusiasm for poetry, and the life which he leads by himself in poetry, it is very difficult to speak. Words cannot easily bring back the pleasure of it, now discerned in the far past like a dream, full of witchery, and music, and adventure. Some children, perhaps the majority, are of such a nature that they weave this dream for themselves, out of their own imaginings, with no aid or with little aid from the poets. Others, possibly less imaginative, if more bookish, gladly accept the poet's help, and are his most flattering readers. There are moments in that remote life which remain always vividly present to memory, as when first we followed the chase with Fitz-James, or first learned how ' The Baron of Smaylho'me rose with day,' or first heard how

> All day long the noise of battle roll'd
> Among the mountains by the winter sea.

Almost the happiest of such moments were those lulled by the sleepy music of ' The Castle of Indolence,' a poem now perhaps seldom read, at least by the young. Yet they may do worse than visit the drowsy castle of him who wrote

> So when a shepherd of the Hebrid isles
> Placed far amid the melancholy main.

Childhood is the age when a love of poetry may be born and strengthened—a taste which grows rarer and more rare in our age, when examinations spring up and choke the good seed. By way of lending no aid to what is called Education, very few notes have been added. The child does not want everything to be explained; in the unexplained is great pleasure. Nothing, perhaps, crushes the love of poetry more surely and swiftly than the use of poems as school-books. They are at once associated in the mind with lessons, with long, with endless hours in school, with puzzling questions and the agony of an imperfect memory, with grammar and etymology, and everything that is the enemy of joy. We may cause children to hate Shakespeare or Spenser as Byron hated Horace, by inflicting poets on them, not for their poetry, but for the valuable information in the notes. This danger, at least, it is not difficult to avoid in the *Blue Poetry Book*.

CONTENTS

CONTENTS

a

LIST OF PLATES

Anthology of Best-Loved Poems

NURSE'S SONG

WHEN the voices of children are heard on the green
  And laughing is heard on the hill,
My heart is at rest within my breast,
  And everything else is still.

Then come home, my children, the sun is gone down,
  And the dews of night arise ;
Come, come, leave off play, and let us away
  Till the morning appears in the skies.

No, no, let us play, for it is yet day,
  And we cannot go to sleep;
Besides in the sky the little birds fly,
  And the hills are all covered with sheep.

Well, well, go and play till the light fades away,
  And then go home to bed.
The little ones leap'd and shouted and laugh'd ;
  And all the hills echoèd.

W. BLAKE.

A BOY'S SONG

WHERE the pools are bright and deep,
Where the grey trout lies asleep,
Up the river and o'er the lea,
That's the way for Billy and me.

Where the blackbird sings the latest,
Where the hawthorn blooms the sweetest
Where the nestlings chirp and flee,
That's the way for Billy and me.

Where the mowers mow the cleanest,
Where the hay lies thick and greenest ;
There to trace the homeward bee,
That's the way for Billy and me.

Where the hazel bank is steepest,
Where the shadow falls the deepest,
Where the clustering nuts fall free,
That's the way for Billy and me.

Why the boys should drive away
Little sweet maidens from the play,
Or love to banter and fight so well,
That's the thing I never could tell.

But this I know, I love to play,
Through the meadow, among the hay ;
Up the water and o'er the lea,
That's the way for Billy and me.

J. HOGG.

I REMEMBER, I REMEMBER

I

I REMEMBER, I remember
 The house where I was born,
The little window where the sun
 Came peeping in at morn ;
He never came a wink too soon,
 Nor brought too long a day,
But now, I often wish the night
 Had borne my breath away !

II

I remember, I remember
 The roses, red and white,
The vi'lets, and the lily-cups,
 Those flowers made of light !
The lilacs where the robin built,
 And where my brother set
The laburnum on his birthday,—
 The tree is living yet !

III

I remember, I remember
 Where I was used to swing,
And thought the air must rush as fresh
 To swallows on the wing ;
My spirit flew in feathers then,
 That is so heavy now,
And summer pools could hardly cool
 The fever on my brow !

IV

I remember, I remember
   The fir trees dark and high ;
I used to think their slender tops
   Were close against the sky :
It was a childish ignorance,
   But now 'tis little joy
To know I'm farther off from heav'n
   Than when I was a boy.

T. HOOD.

THE LAMB

LITTLE Lamb, who made thee ?
Dost thou know who made thee,
Gave thee life, and bid thee feed
By the stream and o'er the mead ;
Gave thee clothing of delight,
Softest clothing, woolly, bright ;
Gave thee such a tender voice
Making all the vales rejoice ;
   Little Lamb, who made thee ?
   Dost thou know who made thee ?

Little Lamb, I'll tell thee.
Little Lamb, I'll tell thee.
He is called by thy name,
For He calls Himself a Lamb :—
He is meek and He is mild ;
He became a little child.
I a child, and thou a lamb,
We are called by His name.
   Little Lamb, God bless thee ;
   Little Lamb, God bless thee.

W. BLAKE.

NIGHT

THE sun descending in the west,
The evening star does shine;
The birds are silent in their nest,
And I must seek for mine.

The moon, like a flower
In heaven's high bower,
With silent delight
Sits and smiles on the night.

Farewell, green fields and happy groves,
  Where flocks have ta'en delight;
Where lambs have nibbled, silent moves
  The feet of angels bright;
    Unseen, they pour blessing,
    And joy without ceasing,
    On each bud and blossom,
    And each sleeping bosom.

They look in every thoughtless nest,
  Where birds are cover'd warm,
They visit caves of every beast,
  To keep them all from harm :—
    If they see any weeping
    That should have been sleeping,
    They pour sleep on their head,
    And sit down by their bed.

                              W. BLAKE.

ON A SPANIEL CALLED 'BEAU' KILLING A YOUNG BIRD

A SPANIEL, Beau, that fares like you,
  Well fed, and at his ease,
Should wiser be than to pursue
  Each trifle that he sees.

But you have killed a tiny bird,
  Which flew not till to-day,
Against my orders, whom you heard
  Forbidding you the prey.

Nor did you kill that you might eat,
   And ease a doggish pain,
For him, though chased with furious heat,
   You left where he was slain.

Nor was he of the thievish sort,
   Or one whom blood allures,
But innocent was all his sport
   Whom you have torn for yours.

My dog! what remedy remains,
   Since, teach you all I can,
I see you, after all my pains,
   So much resemble man?

BEAU'S REPLY

Sir, when I flew to seize the bird
   In spite of your command,
A louder voice than yours I heard,
   And harder to withstand.

You cried—'Forbear!'—but in my breast
   A mightier cried—'Proceed!'—
'Twas Nature, sir, whose strong behest
   Impell'd me to the deed.

Yet much as Nature I respect,
   I ventured once to break
(As you perhaps may recollect)
   Her precept for your sake ;

And when your linnet on a day,
   Passing his prison door,
Had flutter'd all his strength away,
   And panting pressed the floor ;

Well knowing him a sacred thing,
   Not destined to my tooth,
I only kiss'd his ruffled wing,
   And lick'd the feathers smooth.

Let my obedience then excuse
   My disobedience now,
Nor some reproof yourself refuse
   From your aggrieved Bow-wow ;

If killing birds be such a crime,
   (Which I can hardly see),
What think you, sir, of killing Time
   With verse address'd to me ?

                    W. Cowper.

LUCY GRAY; OR, SOLITUDE

Oft I had heard of Lucy Gray :
   And, when I crossed the wild,
I chanced to see at break of day
   The solitary child.

No mate, no comrade Lucy knew ;
   She dwelt on a wide moor,
—The sweetest thing that ever grew
   Beside a human door !

You yet may spy the fawn at play,
　The hare upon the green ;
But the sweet face of Lucy Gray
　Will never more be seen.

' To-night will be a stormy night—
　You to the town must go ;
And take a lantern, Child, to light
　Your mother through the snow.'

' That, Father ! will I gladly do :
　'Tis scarcely afternoon—
The minster-clock has just struck two,
　And yonder is the moon ! '

At this the Father raised his hook,
　And snapped a faggot-band ;
He plied his work ;—and Lucy took
　The lantern in her hand.

Not blither is the mountain roe :
　With many a wanton stroke
Her feet disperse the powdery snow,
　That rises up like smoke.

The storm came on before its time:
  She wandered up and down ;
And many a hill did Lucy climb,
  But never reached the town.

The wretched parents all that night
  Went shouting far and wide;
But there was neither sound nor sight
  To serve them for a guide.

At day-break on a hill they stood
  That overlooked the moor;
And thence they saw the bridge of wood,
  A furlong from their door.

They wept—and, turning homeward, cried,
  ' In heaven we all shall meet!'
—When in the snow the mother spied
  The print of Lucy's feet.

Then downwards from the steep hill's edge
  They tracked the footmarks small;
And through the broken hawthorn hedge,
  And by the long stone wall;

And then an open field they crossed:
  The marks were still the same;
They tracked them on, nor ever lost;
  And to the bridge they came.

They followed from the snowy bank
  Those footmarks, one by one,
Into the middle of the plank;
  And further there were none!

—Yet some maintain that to this day
  She is a living child;
That you may see sweet Lucy Gray
  Upon the lonesome wild.

O'er rough and smooth she trips along,
  And never looks behind;
And sings a solitary song
  That whistles in the wind.

W. WORDSWORTH.

HUNTING SONG

WAKEN, lords and ladies gay!
On the mountain dawns the day;
All the jolly chase is here,
With hawk, and horse, and hunting spear!
Hounds are in their couples yelling,
Hawks are whistling, horns are knelling;
Merrily, merrily, mingle they,
' Waken, lords and ladies gay.'

Waken, lords and ladies gay!
The mist has left the mountain grey,
Springlets in the dawn are steaming,
Diamonds on the brake are gleaming;
And foresters have busy been,
To track the buck in thicket green;
Now we come to chant our lay,
' Waken, lords and ladies gay.'

Waken, lords and ladies gay !
To the greenwood haste away ;
We can show you where he lies,
Fleet of foot, and tall of size;
We can show the marks he made,
When 'gainst the oak his antlers fray'd ;
You shall see him brought to bay—
' Waken, lords and ladies gay.'

Louder, louder chant the lay,
Waken, lords and ladies gay !
Tell them youth, and mirth, and glee,
Run a course as well as we ;
Time, stern huntsman ! who can baulk,
Stanch as hound, and fleet as hawk ?
Think of this, and rise with day,
Gentle lords and ladies gay !

SIR W. SCOTT.

LORD ULLIN'S DAUGHTER

A CHIEFTAIN, to the Highlands bound,
  Cries, ' Boatman, do not tarry !
And I'll give thee a silver pound,
  To row us o'er the ferry.'

' Now who be ye, would cross Lochgyle,
  This dark and stormy water ? '
' O, I'm the chief of Ulva's isle,
  And this Lord Ullin's daughter.—

' And fast before her father's men
  Three days we've fled together,
For should he find us in the glen,
  My blood would stain the heather.

' His horsemen hard behind us ride ;
  Should they our steps discover,
Then who will cheer my bonny bride
  When they have slain her lover ? '

Outspoke the hardy Highland wight,
  ' I'll go, my chief—I'm ready ;
It is not for your silver bright,
  But for your winsome lady :

' And by my word ! the bonny bird
  In danger shall not tarry ;
So though the waves are raging white,
  I'll row you o'er the ferry.'—

By this the storm grew loud apace,
  The water-wraith was shrieking ;[1]
And in the scowl of heaven each face
  Grew dark as they were speaking.

But still as wilder blew the wind,
  And as the night grew drearer,
Adown the glen rode armèd men,
  Their trampling sounded nearer.—

' O haste thee, haste ! ' the lady cries,
  ' Though tempests round us gather ;
I'll meet the raging of the skies,
  But not an angry father.'—

The boat has left a stormy land,
  A stormy sea before her,—
When, oh ! too strong for human hand,
  The tempest gather'd o'er her.

And still they row'd amidst the roar
  Of waters fast prevailing :
Lord Ullin reach'd that fatal shore,
  His wrath was changed to wailing.—

For sore dismay'd, through storm and shade,
  His child he did discover :—
One lovely hand she stretch'd for aid,
  And one was round her lover.

---

[1] The evil spirit of the waters,

'Come back ! come back ! ' he cried in grief,
 ' Across this stormy water :
And I'll forgive your Highland chief,
 My daughter !—oh my daughter ! '—

'Twas vain : the loud waves lashed the shore,
  Return or aid preventing ;—
The waters wild went o'er his child,—
  And he was left lamenting.

T. CAMPBELL.

THE CHIMNEY-SWEEPER

WHEN my mother died I was very young,
And my father sold me while yet my tongue
Could scarcely cry, ' *'weep ! 'weep ! 'weep ! 'weep !* '
So your chimneys I sweep, and in soot I sleep.

There's little Tom Dacre, who cried when his head,
That curl'd like a lamb's back, was shaved ; so I said,
' Hush, Tom ! never mind it, for when your head's bare,
You know that the soot cannot spoil your white hair.'

And so he was quiet : and that very night,
As Tom was a-sleeping, he had such a sight,
That thousands of sweepers, Dick, Joe, Ned, and Jack,
Were all of them lock'd up in coffins of black.

And by came an angel, who had a bright key,
And he open'd the coffins, and set them all free ;
Then down a green plain, leaping, laughing they run,
And wash in a river, and shine in the sun.

Then, naked and white, all their bags left behind,
They rise upon clouds, and sport in the wind ;
And the angel told Tom, if he'd be a good boy,
He'd have God for his father, and never want joy.

And so Tom awoke ; and we rose in the dark,
And got with our bags and our brushes to work ;
Though the morning was cold, Tom was happy and warm :
So, if all do their duty, they need not fear harm.

W. BLAKE.

NORA'S VOW

I

HEAR what Highland Nora said,—
' The Earlie's son I will not wed,
Should all the race of nature die,
And none be left but he and I.
For all the gold, for all the gear,
And all the lands both far and near,
That ever valour lost or won,
I would not wed the Earlie's son.'

I

' A maiden's vows,' old Callum spoke,
' Are lightly made, and lightly broke ;
The heather on the mountain's height
Begins to bloom in purple light ;

C

The frost-wind soon shall sweep away
That lustre deep from glen and brae ;
Yet Nora, ere its bloom be gone,
May blithely wed the Earlie's son.'—

III

' The swan,' she said, ' the lake's clear breast
May barter for the eagle's nest ;
The Awe's fierce stream may backward turn,
Ben-Cruaichan fall, and crush Kilchurn ;
Our kilted clans, when blood is high,
Before their foes may turn and fly ;
But I, were all these marvels done,
Would never wed the Earlie's son.'

IV

Still in the water-lily's shade
Her wonted nest the wild-swan made ;
Ben-Cruaichan stands as fast as ever,
Still downward foams the Awe's fierce river ;
To shun the clash of foeman's steel,
No Highland brogue has turn'd the heel :
But Nora's heart is lost and won,
—She's wedded to the Earlie's son !

SIR W. SCOTT.

BALLAD OF AGINCOURT

FAIR stood the wind for France,
When we our sails advance,
Nor now to prove our chance
    Longer will tarry ;
But putting to the main,
At Caux, the mouth of Seine,
With all his martial train,
    Landed King Harry.

And, taking many a fort,
Furnished in warlike sort,
Marcheth tow'rds Agincourt
    In happy hour,
(Skirmishing day by day,
With those oppose his way)
Where the French general lay
    With all his power.

Which in his height of pride,
King Henry to deride,
His ransom to provide
    To the king sending;

And, turning to his men,
Quoth our brave Henry then:
Though they to one be ten,
    Be not amazed!

Which he neglects the while,
As from a nation vile,
Yet with an angry smile
    Their fall portending,

Yet have we well begun;
Battles so bravely won,
Have ever to the sun
    By fame been raisèd.

And for myself (quoth he),—
This my full rest shall be,
England ne'er mourn for me,
    Nor more esteem me ;—
Victor I will remain,
Or on this earth lie slain :
Never shall she sustain
    Loss to redeem me.

Poitiers and Cressy tell,
When most their pride did swell,
Under our swords they fell ;
    No less our skill is
Than when our grandsire great,
Claiming the regal seat,
By many a warlike feat
    Lopp'd the French lilies.

The Duke of York so dread
The eager vanward led,
With the main Henry sped,
    Amongst his henchmen.
Exceter had the rear,
A braver man not there,—
O Lord ! how hot they were,
    On the false Frenchmen !

They now to fight are gone :
Armour on armour shone,
Drum now to drum did groan—
    To hear was wonder ;
That with the cries they make,
The very earth did shake ;
Trumpet to trumpet spake --
    Thunder to thunder.

Well it thine age became,
O noble Erpingham !
Which didst the signal aim
    To our hid forces,—

When from a meadow by,
Like a storm suddenly,
The English archery
    Stuck the French horses.

With Spanish yew so strong,
Arrows a cloth-yard long,
That like to serpents stung,
    Piercing the weather,—
None from his fellow starts,
But, playing manly parts,
And like true English hearts
    Stuck close together.

When down their bows they
    threw,
And forth their bilboes drew,
And on the French they flew,
    Not one was tardy ;
Arms from the shoulders sent,
Scalps to the teeth were rent,
Down the French peasants
    went,—
    Our men were hardy.

This while our noble king,
His broadsword brandishing,
Into the host did fling,
    As to o'erwhelm it,
And many a deep wound lent,
His arms with blood besprent,
And many a cruel dent
    Bruizèd his helmet.

Gloster, that duke so good,
Next of the royal blood,
For famous England stood,
    With his brave brother ;
Clarence, in steel so bright,
Though but a maiden knight
Yet in that furious fight
    Scarce such another.

Warwick in blood did wade ;
Oxford the foe invade,
And cruel slaughter made
    Still as they ran up ;

Upon Saint Crispin's day
Fought was this noble fray,
Which fame did not delay
    To England to carry.

Suffolk his axe did ply ;
Beaumont and Willoughby
Bare them right doughtily,
    Ferrars and Fanhope.

O when shall Englishmen,
With such acts fill a pen,
Or England breed again
    Such a King Harry ?

              M. Drayton.

YE MARINERS OF ENGLAND

A NAVAL ODE

I

Ye Mariners of England !
That guard our native seas ;
Whose flag has braved, a thousand years,
The battle and the breeze !
Your glorious standard launch again
To meet another foe !
And sweep through the deep,
While the stormy tempests blow ;
While the battle rages loud and long,
And the stormy tempests blow.

I

The spirits of your fathers
Shall start from every wave !—
For the deck it was their field of fame,
And Ocean was their grave :
Where Blake and mighty Nelson fell,
Your manly hearts shall glow,
As ye sweep through the deep,
While the stormy tempests blow
While the battle rages loud and long,
And the stormy tempests blow.

III

Britannia needs no bulwark,
No towers along the steep ;
Her march is o'er the mountain-waves,
Her home is on the deep.
With thunders from her native oak
She quells the floods below,—
As they roar on the shore,
When the stormy tempests blow ;
When the battle rages loud and long,
And the stormy tempests blow.

AND THE STAR OF PEACE RETURN.

IV

The meteor flag of England
Shall yet terrific burn;
Till danger's troubled night depart,
And the star of peace return.
Then, then, ye ocean-warriors!
Our song and feast shall flow
To the fame of your name,
When the storm has ceased to blow;
When the fiery fight is heard no more,
And the storm has ceased to blow.

T. CAMPBELL.

THE GIRL DESCRIBES HER FAWN

WITH sweetest milk and sugar first
I it at my own fingers nursed;
And as it grew, so every day
It wax'd more white and sweet than they.
It had so sweet a breath! and oft
I blush'd to see its foot more soft
And white, shall I say, than my hand?
Nay, any lady's of the land!
It is a wond'rous thing how fleet
'Twas on those little silver feet:
With what a pretty skipping grace
It oft would challenge me the race;
And when 't had left me far away
'Twould stay, and run again, and stay,
For it was nimbler much than hinds;
And trod as if on the four winds.

I have a garden of my own,
But so with roses overgrown,
And lilies, that you would it guess
To be a little wilderness,

And all the springtime of the year
It only lovèd to be there.
Among the beds of lilies I
Have sought it oft, where it should lie;
Yet could not, till itself would rise,
Find it, although before mine eyes.
For, in the flaxen lilies' shade
It like a bank of lilies laid.
Upon the roses it would feed,
Until its lips e'en seem'd to bleed;

And then to me 'twould boldly trip,
And print those roses on my lip.
But all its chief delight was still
On roses thus itself to fill;
And its pure virgin limbs to fold
In whitest sheets of lilies cold.
Had it lived long, it would have been
Lilies without, roses within.

A. MARVELL.

THE SOLDIER'S DREAM

OUR bugles sang truce, for the night-cloud had lower'd,
  And the sentinel stars set their watch in the sky;
And thousands had sunk on the ground overpower'd,
  The weary to sleep, and the wounded to die.

When reposing that night on my pallet of straw
  By the wolf-scaring faggot that guarded the slain,
At the dead of the night a sweet Vision I saw;
  And thrice ere the morning I dreamt it again.

Methought from the battle-field's dreadful array
  Far, far, I had roam'd on a desolate track:
'Twas Autumn,—and sunshine arose on the way
  To the home of my fathers, that welcomed me back.

I flew to the pleasant fields traversed so oft
  In life's morning march, when my bosom was young;
I heard my own mountain-goats bleating aloft,
  And knew the sweet strain that the corn-reapers sung.

Then pledged we the wine-cup, and fondly I swore
  From my home and my weeping friends never to part;
My little ones kiss'd me a thousand times o'er,
  And my wife sobb'd aloud in her fulness of heart.

'Stay—stay with us!—rest!—thou art weary and worn!'—
  And fain was their war-broken soldier to stay;—
But sorrow return'd with the dawning of morn,
  And the voice in my dreaming ear melted away.

T. CAMPBELL.

JOHN GILPIN

John Gilpin was a citizen
  Of credit and renown,
A train-band Captain eke was he
  Of famous London town.

John Gilpin's spouse said to her dear,
  Though wedded we have been
These twice ten tedious years, yet we
  No holiday have seen.

To-morrow is our wedding-day,
  And we will then repair
Unto the Bell at Edmonton,
  All in a chaise and pair.

My sister and my sister's child,
  Myself, and children three,
Will fill the chaise; so you must ride
  On horseback after we.

He soon replied,—I do admire
  Of womankind but one,
And you are she, my dearest dear,
  Therefore it shall be done.

I am a linendraper bold,
  As all the world doth know,
And my good friend, the Callender,
  Will lend his horse to go.

Quoth Mistress Gilpin,—That's well said;
  And for that wine is dear,
We will be furnish'd with our own,
  Which is both bright and clear.

John Gilpin kiss'd his loving wife;
    O'erjoy'd was he to find
That though on pleasure she was bent,
    She had a frugal mind.

The morning came, the chaise was brought,
    But yet was not allow'd
To drive up to the door, lest all
    Should say that she was proud.

So three doors off the chaise was stay'd,
    Where they did all get in,
Six precious souls, and all agog
    To dash through thick and thin.

Smack went the whip, round went the wheels;
    Were never folks so glad,
The stones did rattle underneath,
    As if Cheapside were mad.

John Gilpin at his horse's side,
    Seized fast the flowing mane,
And up he got in haste to ride,
    But soon came down again.

For saddle-tree scarce reach'd had he,
    His journey to begin,
When turning round his head he saw
    Three customers come in.

So down he came, for loss of time
    Although it grieved him sore,
Yet loss of pence, full well he knew,
    Would trouble him much more.

'Twas long before the customers
    Were suited to their mind,
When Betty screaming came downstairs,
    The wine is left behind.

Good lack ! quoth he, yet bring it me,
  My leathern belt likewise
In which I bear my trusty sword
  When I do exercise.

Now Mistress Gilpin, careful soul,
  Had two stone bottles found,
To hold the liquor that she loved,
  And keep it safe and sound.

Each bottle had a curling ear,
  Through which the belt he drew,
And hung a bottle on each side
  To make his balance true.

Then over all, that he might be
  Equipp'd from top to toe,
His long red cloak well-brush'd and neat,
  He manfully did throw.

Now see him mounted once again
  Upon his nimble steed,
Full slowly pacing o'er the stones,
  With caution and good heed.

But finding soon a smoother road
  Beneath his well-shod feet,
The snorting beast began to trot,
  Which gall'd him in his seat.

So, Fair and softly ! John he cried,
  But John he cried in vain ;
That trot became a gallop soon,
  In spite of curb and rein.

So stooping down, as needs he must
  Who cannot sit upright,
He grasp'd the mane with both his hands
  And eke with all his might.

His horse, who never in that sort
　　Had handled been before,
What thing upon his back had got
　　Did wonder more and more.

Away went Gilpin neck or nought,
　　Away went hat and wig ;
He little dreamt, when he set out,
　　Of running such a rig.

The wind did blow, the cloak did fly,
　　Like streamer long and gay,
Till, loop and button failing both,
　　At last it flew away.

Then might all people well discern
　　The bottles he had slung ;
A bottle swinging at each side
　　As hath been said or sung.

The dogs did bark, the children scream'd,
　　Up flew the windows all,
And every soul cried out, Well done !
　　As loud as he could bawl.

Away went Gilpin—who but he ?
　　His fame soon spread around,
He carries weight, he rides a race,
　　'Tis for a thousand pound.

And still as fast as he drew near,
　　'Twas wonderful to view
How in a trice the turnpike-men
　　Their gates wide open threw.

And now as he went bowing down
　　His reeking head full low,
The bottles twain behind his back
　　Were shatter'd at a blow.

Down ran the wine into the road
  Most piteous to be seen,
Which made his horse's flanks to smoke
  As they had basted been.

But still he seem'd to carry weight,
  With leathern girdle braced,
For all might see the bottle-necks
  Still dangling at his waist.

Thus all through merry Islington
  These gambols he did play,
And till he came unto the Wash
  Of Edmonton so gay.

And there he threw the Wash about
  On both sides of the way,
Just like unto a trundling mop,
  Or a wild-goose at play.

At Edmonton his loving wife
  From the balcòny spied
Her tender husband, wondering much
  To see how he did ride.

Stop, stop, John Gilpin !—Here's the house—
  They all at once did cry,
The dinner waits, and we are tired ;
  Said Gilpin—So am I !

But yet his horse was not a whit
  Inclined to tarry there,
For why ? his owner had a house
  Full ten miles off, at Ware.

So like an arrow swift he flew
  Shot by an archer strong,
So did he fly—which brings me to
  The middle of my song.

Away went Gilpin, out of breath,
 And sore against his will,
Till at his friend the Callender's
 His horse at last stood still.

The Callender, amazed to see
 His neighbour in such trim,
Laid down his pipe, flew to the gate,
 And thus accosted him—

What news? what news? your tidings tell,
 Tell me you must and shall—
Say, why bareheaded you are come,
 Or why you come at all?

Now Gilpin had a pleasant wit,
 And loved a timely joke,
And thus unto the Callender
 In merry guise he spoke—

I came because your horse would come;
 And if I well forbode,
My hat and wig will soon be here,
 They are upon the road.

The Callender, right glad to find
 His friend in merry pin,
Return'd him not a single word,
 But to the house went in.

Whence straight he came with hat and wig,
 A wig that flow'd behind,
A hat not much the worse for wear,
 Each comely in its kind.

He held them up, and in his turn
 Thus show'd his ready wit,
 My head is twice as big as yours,
 They therefore needs must fit.

But let me scrape the dirt away,
  That hangs upon your face ;
And stop and eat, for well you may
  Be in a hungry case.

Said John—It is my wedding-day,
  And all the world would stare,
If wife should dine at Edmonton
  And I should dine at Ware.

So, turning to his horse, he said,
  I am in haste to dine,
'Twas for your pleasure you came here,
  You shall go back for mine.

Ah, luckless speech, and bootless boast !
  For which he paid full dear,
For while he spake a braying ass
  Did sing most loud and clear.

Whereat his horse did snort as he
  Had heard a lion roar,
And gallop'd off with all his might,
  As he had done before.

Away went Gilpin, and away
  Went Gilpin's hat and wig ;
He lost them sooner than at first,
  For why ? they were too big.

Now Mistress Gilpin, when she saw
  Her husband posting down
Into the country far away,
  She pull'd out half-a-crown ;

And thus unto the youth she said,
  That drove them to the Bell,
This shall be yours, when you bring back
  My husband safe and well.

The youth did ride, and soon did meet
  John coming back amain,
Whom in a trice he tried to stop
  By catching at his rein.

But not performing what he meant,
  And gladly would have done,
The frighten'd steed he frighten'd more
  And made him faster run.

Away went Gilpin, and away
  Went postboy at his heels,
The postboy's horse right glad to miss
  The lumbering of the wheels.

Six gentlemen upon the road
  Thus seeing Gilpin fly,
With postboy scampering in the rear,
  They raised the hue and cry.

Stop thief!—stop thief!—a highwayman!
  Not one of them was mute,
And all and each that pass'd that way
  Did join in the pursuit.

And now the turnpike gates again
  Flew open in short space,
The toll-men thinking as before
  That Gilpin rode a race.

And so he did and won it too,
  For he got first to town,
Nor stopp'd till where he had got up
  He did again get down.

—Now let us sing, Long live the king,
  And Gilpin long live he,
And when he next doth ride abroad,
  May I be there to see!

W. Cowper.

HOHENLINDEN

On Linden, when the sun was low,
All bloodless lay th' untrodden snow;
And dark as winter was the flow
    Of Iser, rolling rapidly.

But Linden saw another sight,
When the drum beat, at dead of night
Commanding fires of death to light
    The darkness of her scenery.

By torch and trumpet fast array'd
Each horseman drew his battle-blade,
And furious every charger neigh'd
    To join the dreadful revelry.

Then shook the hills with thunder riven;
Then rush'd the steed to battle driven,
And louder than the bolts of Heaven,
    Far flash'd the red artillery.

But redder yet that light shall glow
On Linden's hills of stainèd snow;
And bloodier yet the torrent flow
    Of Iser, rolling rapidly.

'Tis morn, but scarce yon level sun
Can pierce the war-clouds, rolling dun,
Where furious Frank, and fiery Hun,
    Shout in their sulph'rous canopy.

The combat deepens. On, ye brave
Who rush to glory, or the grave!
Wave, Munich! all thy banners wave,
    And charge with all thy chivalry!

Few, few, shall part, where many meet!
The snow shall be their winding-sheet,
And every turf beneath their feet
    Shall be a soldier's sepulchre.

T. CAMPBELL.

THE VILLAGE BLACKSMITH

UNDER a spreading chestnut tree
    The village smithy stands;
The smith, a mighty man is he,
    With large and sinewy hands;
And the muscles of his brawny arms
    Are strong as iron bands.

His hair is crisp, and black, and long,
    His face is like the tan;
His brow is wet with honest sweat,
    He earns whate'er he can,
And looks the whole world in the face,
    For he owes not any man.

Week in, week out, from morn till night,
    You can hear his bellows blow;
You can hear him swing his heavy sledge,
    With measured beat and slow,
Like a sexton ringing the village bell,
    When the evening sun is low.

And children coming home from school
    Look in at the open door;
They love to see the flaming forge,
    And hear the bellows roar,
And catch the burning sparks that fly
    Like chaff from a threshing-floor.

He goes on Sunday to the church,
    And sits among his boys;
He hears the parson pray and preach,
    He hears his daughter's voice,
Singing in the village choir,
    And it makes his heart rejoice.

It sounds to him like her mother's voice,
    Singing in Paradise !
He needs must think of her once more,
    How in the grave she lies ;
And with his hard, rough hand he wipes
    A tear out of his eyes.

Toiling,—rejoicing,—sorrowing,
    Onward through life he goes ;
Each morning sees some task begin,
    Each evening sees it close ;
Something attempted, something done,
    Has earned a night's repose.

Thanks, thanks to thee, my worthy friend,
    For the lesson thou hast taught !
Thus at the flaming forge of life
    Our fortunes must be wrought ;
Thus on its sounding anvil shaped
    Each burning deed and thought !

H. W. LONGFELLOW.

ELEGY ON THE DEATH OF A MAD DOG

GOOD people all, of every sort,
    Give ear unto my song ;
And if you find it wondrous short,
    It cannot hold you long.

In Islington there was a Man,
    Of whom the world might say,
That still a godly race he ran,
    Whene'er he went to pray.

A kind and gentle heart he had,
    To comfort friends and foes,
The naked every day he clad,
    When he put on his clothes.

And in that town a Dog was found,
   As many dogs there be,
Both mongrel, puppy, whelp, and hound,
   And curs of low degree.

This Dog and Man at first were friends;
   But when a pique began,
The Dog, to gain some private ends,
   Went mad and bit the Man.

Around from all the neighbouring streets
   The wond'ring neighbours ran,
And swore the Dog had lost his wits,
   To bite so good a Man.

The wound it seem'd both sore and sad
    To every Christian eye;
And while they swore the Dog was mad,
    They swore the Man would die.

But soon a wonder came to light,
    That show'd the rogues they lied:
The Man recover'd of the bite,
    The Dog it was that died.

O. GOLDSMITH.

THE OUTLAW

O, BRIGNALL banks are wild and fair,
    And Greta woods are green,
And you may gather garlands there
    Would grace a summer queen.
And as I rode by Dalton Hall
    Beneath the turrets high,
A Maiden on the castle wall
    Was singing merrily,—

' O, Brignall banks are fresh and fair,
    And Greta woods are green ;
I'd rather rove with Edmund there,
    Than reign our English queen.'

—' If, Maiden, thou wouldst wend with me,
    To leave both tower and town,
Thou first must guess what life lead we,
    That dwell by dale and down ?

And if thou canst that riddle read,
    As read full well you may,
Then to the greenwood shalt thou speed
    As blithe as Queen of May.'
Yet sung she, ' Brignall banks are fair,
    And Greta woods are green ;
I'd rather rove with Edmund there
    Than reign our English queen.'

' I read you by your bugle horn
   And by your palfrey good,
I read you for a Ranger sworn,
   To keep the king's greenwood.'
—' A Ranger, lady, winds his horn,
   And 'tis at peep of light ;
His blast is heard at merry morn,
   And mine at dead of night.'
Yet sung she, ' Brignall banks are fair,
   And Greta woods are gay ;
I would I were with Edmund there,
   To reign his Queen of May !

'With burnish'd brand and musketoon,
   So gallantly you come,
I read you for a bold Dragoon
   That lists the tuck of drum.'
—' I list no more the tuck of drum,
   No more the trumpet hear ;
But when the beetle sounds his hum,
   My comrades take the spear.
And O ! though Brignall banks be fair
   And Greta woods be gay,
Yet mickle must the maiden dare,
   Would reign my Queen of May !

' Maiden ! a nameless life I lead,
   A nameless death I'll die !
The fiend, whose lantern lights the mead
   Were better mate than I !
And when I'm with my comrades met
   Beneath the greenwood bough,
What once we were we all forget,
   Nor think what we are now.'

CHORUS

Yet Brignall banks are fresh and fair,
   And Greta woods are green,
And you may gather garlands there
   Would grace a summer queen.

Sir W. Scott.

BATTLE OF THE BALTIC

Of Nelson and the North,
Sing the glorious day's renown,
When to battle fierce came forth
All the might of Denmark's crown,
And her arms along the deep proudly shone;
By each gun the lighted brand,
In a bold determined hand,
And the Prince of all the land
Led them on.—

Like leviathans afloat,
Lay their bulwarks on the brine;
While the sign of battle flew
On the lofty British line:
It was ten of April morn by the chime:
As they drifted on their path,
There was silence deep as death;
And the boldest held his breath
For a time.—

But the might of England flush'd
To anticipate the scene;
And her van the fleeter rush'd
O'er the deadly space between.
'Hearts of oak!' our captains cried, when each gun
From its adamantine lips
Spread a death-shade round the ships,
Like the hurricane eclipse
Of the sun.

Again! again! again!
And the havoc did not slack,
Till a feeble cheer the Dane
To our cheering sent us back;—
Their shots along the deep slowly boom:—
Then ceased—and all is wail,
As they strike the shatter'd sail;
Or, in conflagration pale,
Light the gloom.

Out spoke the victor then
As he hail'd them o'er the wave;
'Ye are brothers! ye are men!
And we conquer but to save:—
So peace instead of death let us bring;
But yield, proud foe, thy fleet
With the crews, at England's feet,
And make submission meet
To our King.'

Then Denmark bless'd our chief
That he gave her wounds repose;
And the sounds of joy and grief
From her people wildly rose,
As death withdrew his shades from the day.
While the sun look'd smiling bright
O'er a wide and woeful sight,
Where the fires of funeral light
Died away.

Now joy, old England, raise!
For the tidings of thy might,
By the festal cities' blaze,
Whilst the wine-cup shines in light;
And yet amidst that joy and uproar,
Let us think of them that sleep,
Full many a fathom deep,
By thy wild and stormy steep,
Elsinore!

Brave hearts! to Britain's pride
Once so faithful and so true,
On the deck of fame that died;
With the gallant good Riou;
Soft sigh the winds of heaven o'er their grave!
While the billow mournful rolls,
And the mermaid's song condoles,
Singing Glory to the souls
Of the brave!

                                        T. Campbell.

YOUNG LOCHINVAR

O, YOUNG Lochinvar is come out of the West!
Through all the wide Border his steed was the best;
And save his good broadsword, he weapons had none;
He rode all unarm'd, and he rode all alone.
So faithful in love, and so dauntless in war,
There never was knight like the young Lochinvar.

He stay'd not for brake and he stopp'd not for stone;
He swam the Eske river where ford there was none;
But ere he alighted at Netherby gate,
The bride had consented, the gallant came late;
For a laggard in love, and a dastard in war,
Was to wed the fair Ellen of brave Lochinvar.

So boldly he enter'd the Netherby Hall,
Among bridesmen, and kinsmen, and brothers, and all;—
Then spoke the bride's father, his hand on his sword
(For the poor craven bridegroom said never a word),
'O, come ye in peace here, or come ye in war,
Or to dance at our bridal, young Lord Lochinvar?

'I long woo'd your daughter, my suit you denied;—
Love swells like the Solway, but ebbs like its tide;—
And now am I come with this lost Love of mine
To lead but one measure, drink one cup of wine.
There are maidens in Scotland more lovely by far,
That would gladly be bride to the young Lochinvar!'

The bride kiss'd the goblet: the knight took it up,
He quaff'd off the wine and he threw down the cup.
She look'd down to blush, and she look'd up to sigh,
With a smile on her lips, and a tear in her eye.
He took her soft hand, ere her mother could bar,—
'Now tread we a measure!' said young Lochinvar.

So stately his form, and so lovely her face,
That never a hall such a galliard did grace;
While her mother did fret, and her father did fume,
And the bridegroom stood dangling his bonnet and plume;
And the bride-maidens whispered, ' 'Twere better by far,
To have match'd our fair cousin with young Lochinvar ! '

One touch to her hand, and one word in her ear,
When they reach'd the hall door; and the charger stood near;
So light to the croupe the fair lady he swung,
So light to the saddle before her he sprung!
'She is won ! we are gone, over bank, bush, and scaur;
They'll have fleet steeds that follow,' quoth young Lochinvar.

There was mounting 'mong Græmes of the Netherby clan,
Forsters, Fenwicks, and Musgraves, they rode and they ran
There was racing and chasing, on Cannobie lea,
But the lost bride of Netherby ne'er did they see.
So daring in love, and so dauntless in war,
Have ye e'er heard of gallant like young Lochinvar ?

Sir W. Scott.

THE WRECK OF THE HESPERUS

It was the schooner Hesperus,
    That sailed the wintry sea;
And the skipper had taken his little daughter,
    To bear him company.

Blue were her eyes as the fairy-flax,
    Her cheeks like the dawn of day,
And her bosom white as the hawthorn buds,
    That ope in the month of May.

The skipper he stood beside the helm,
    His pipe was in his mouth,
And he watched how the veering flaw did blow
    The smoke now West, now South.

Then up and spake an old sailòr,
    Had sail'd the Spanish Main,
'I pray thee, put into yonder port,
    For I fear a hurricane.

'Last night, the moon had a golden ring,
    And to-night no moon we see!'
The skipper, he blew a whiff from his pipe,
    And a scornful laugh laughed he.

Colder and louder blew the wind,
    A gale from the North-east;
The snow fell hissing in the brine,
    And the billows frothed like yeast.

Down came the storm, and smote amain
    The vessel in its strength;
She shudder'd and paused. like a frighted steed,
    Then leap'd her cable's length.

'Come hither! come hither! my little daughtèr,
    And do not tremble so;
For I can weather the roughest gale
    That ever wind did blow.'

He wrapp'd her warm in his seaman's coat
    Against the stinging blast;
He cut a rope from a broken spar,
    And bound her to the mast.

'O father! I hear the church-bells ring,
    'O say, what may it be?'
''Tis a fog-bell, on a rock-bound coast!'—
    And he steer'd for the open sea.

'O father! I hear the sound of guns,
    O say, what may it be?'
'Some ship in distress that cannot live
    In such an angry sea!'

' O father ! I see a gleaming light,
   O say, what may it be ? '
But the father answered never a word,
   A frozen corpse was he.

Lashed to the helm, all stiff and stark,
   With his face turned to the skies,
The lantern gleamed through the gleaming snow
   On his fixed and glassy eyes.

Then the maiden clasped her hands and prayed
   That savèd she might be ;
And she thought of Christ, who stilled the waves
   On the Lake of Galilee.

And fast through the midnight dark and drear,
  Through the whistling sleet and snow,
Like a sheeted ghost, the vessel swept
  Towards the reef of Norman's Woe.

And ever the fitful gusts between
  A sound came from the land ;
It was the sound of the trampling surf,
  On the rocks and the hard sea-sand.

The breakers were right beneath her bows,
  She drifted a dreary wreck,
And a whooping billow swept the crew
  Like icicles from her deck.

She struck where the white and fleecy waves
  Look'd soft as carded wool,
But the cruel rocks, they gored her sides
  Like the horns of an angry bull.

Her rattling shrouds, all sheathed in ice,
  With the masts went by the board ;
Like a vessel of glass, she stove and sank,
  Ho ! ho ! the breakers roared !

At day-break, on the bleak sea-beach
  A fisherman stood aghast,
To see the form of a maiden fair
  Lashed close to a drifting mast.

The salt sea was frozen on her breast,
  The salt tears in her eyes ;
And he saw her hair like the brown sea-weed
  On the billows fall and rise.

Such was the wreck of the Hesperus,
  In the midnight and the snow !
Christ save us all from a death like this,
  On the reef of Norman's Woe !

                              H. W. LONGFELLOW.

E

THE DOG AND THE WATER-LILY

The noon was shady, and soft airs
　　Swept Ouse's silent tide,
When, 'scaped from literary cares,
　　I wander'd on his side.

My spaniel, prettiest of his race,
　　And high in pedigree,—
(Two nymphs adorn'd with every grace
　　That spaniel found for me,)

Now wanton'd lost in flags and reeds,
　　Now, starting into sight,
Pursued the swallow o'er the meads
　　With scarce a slower flight.

It was the time when Ouse display'd
　　His lilies newly blown;
Their beauties I intent survey'd,
　　And one I wish'd my own.

With cane extended far I sought
　　To steer it close to land;
But still the prize, though nearly caught,
　　Escaped my eager hand.

Beau mark'd my unsuccessful pains
　　With fix'd considerate face,
And puzzling set his puppy brains
　　To comprehend the case.

But with a cherup clear and strong
　　Dispersing all his dream,
I thence withdrew, and follow'd long
　　The windings of the stream.

My ramble ended, I return'd ;
  Beau, trotting far before,
The floating wreath again discern'd,
  And plunging left the shore.

I saw him with that lily cropp'd
  Impatient swim to meet
My quick approach, and soon he dropp'd
  The treasure at my feet.

Charm'd with the sight, ' The world,' I cried,
  Shall hear of this thy deed ;
My dog shall mortify the pride
  Of man's superior breed ;

' But chief myself I will enjoin,
  Awake at duty's call,
To show a love as prompt as thine
  To Him who gives me all.'

W. COWPER.

TO FLUSH, MY DOG

LOVING friend, the gift of one,
Who her own true faith hath run
  Through thy lower nature ;
Be my benediction said
With my hand upon thy head,
  Gentle fellow-creature !

Like a lady's ringlets brown,
Flow thy silken ears adown
  Either side demurely,
Of thy silver-suited breast
Shining out from all the rest
  Of thy body purely.

E 2

Darkly brown thy body is,
Till the sunshine, striking this,
   Alchemise its dulness,—
When the sleek curls manifold ·
Flash all over into gold,
   With a burnished fulness.

Underneath my stroking hand,
Startled eyes of hazel bland
   Kindling, growing larger,—
Up thou leapest with a spring,
Full of prank and curvetting,
   Leaping like a charger.

Leap! thy broad tail waves a light;
Leap! thy slender feet are bright,
   Canopied in fringes.
Leap—those tasselled ears of thine
Flicker strangely, fair and fine,
   Down their golden inches.

Yet, my pretty sportive friend,
Little is't to such an end
   That I praise thy rareness!
Other dogs may be thy peers
Haply in these drooping ears,
   And this glossy fairness.

But of *thee* it shall be said,
This dog watched beside a bed
   Day and night unweary,—
Watched within a curtained room,
Where no sunbeam brake the gloom
   Round the sick and dreary.

Roses, gathered for a vase,
In that chamber died apace,
   Beam and breeze resigning—
This dog only, waited on,
Knowing that when light is gone,
   Love remains for shining.

Other dogs in thymy dew
Tracked the hares and followed through
    Sunny moor or meadow—
This dog only, crept and crept
Next a languid cheek that slept,
    Sharing in the shadow.

Other dogs of loyal cheer
Bounded at the whistle clear,
    Up the woodside hieing—
This dog only, watched in reach
Of a faintly uttered speech,
    Or a louder sighing.

And if one or two quick tears
Dropped upon his glossy ears,
    Or a sigh came double,—
Up he sprang in eager haste,
Fawning, fondling, breathing fast,
    In a tender trouble.

And this dog was satisfied,
If a pale thin hand would glide,
    Down his dewlaps sloping,—
Which he pushed his nose within,
After,—platforming his chin
    On the palm left open.

This dog, if a friendly voice
Call him now to blyther choice
    Than such chamber-keeping,
' Come out ! ' praying from the door,
Presseth backward as before,
    Up against me leaping.

Therefore to this dog will I,
Tenderly not scornfully,
    Render praise and favour !
With my hand upon his head,
Is my benediction said
    Therefore, and for ever.

And because he loves me so,
Better than his kind will do
   Often, man or woman,—
Give I back more love again
Than dogs often take of men,—
   Leaning from my Human.

Blessings on thee, dog of mine,
Pretty collars make thee fine,
   Sugared milk make fat thee!
Pleasures wag on in thy tail—
Hands of gentle motions fail
   Nevermore, to pat thee!

Downy pillow take thy head,
Silken coverlid bestead,
   Sunshine help thy sleeping!
No fly's buzzing wake thee up—
No man break thy purple cup,
   Set for drinking deep in.

Whiskered cats arointed flee—
Sturdy stoppers keep from thee
   Cologne distillations!
Nuts lie in thy path for stones,
And thy feast-day macaroons
   Turn to daily rations!

Mock I thee, in wishing weal?—
Tears are in my eyes to feel
   Thou art made so straitly,
Blessing needs must straiten too,—
Little canst thou joy or do,
   Thou who lovest *greatly*.

Yet be blessed to the height
Of all good and all delight
   Pervious to thy nature,—
Only *loved* beyond that line,
With a love that answers thine,
   Loving fellow-creature!

                    Mrs. Browning.

ALICE BRAND

I

MERRY it is in the good greenwood,
  When the mavis and merle are singing,
When the deer sweeps by, and the hounds are in cry,
  And the hunter's horn is ringing.

' O Alice Brand, my native land
  Is lost for love of you;
And we must hold by wood and wold,
  As outlaws wont to do!

' O Alice, 'twas all for thy locks so bright,
  And 'twas all for thine eyes so blue,
That on the night of our luckless flight,
  Thy brother bold I slew.

' Now must I teach to hew the beech,
  The hand that held the glaive,
For leaves to spread our lowly bed,
  And stakes to fence our cave.

' And for vest of pall, thy fingers small,
  That wont on harp to stray,
A cloak must shear from the slaughter'd deer,
  To keep the cold away.'—

—' O Richard! if my brother died,
  'Twas but a fatal chance:
For darkling was the battle tried,
  And fortune sped the lance.

' If pall and vair no more I wear,
  Nor thou the crimson sheen,
As warm, we'll say, is the russet gray;
  As gay the forest-green.

' And, Richard, if our lot be hard,
　　And lost thy native land,
Still Alice has her own Richàrd,
　　And he his Alice Brand.'

II

'Tis merry, 'tis merry, in good greenwood,
　　So blithe Lady Alice is singing;
On the beech's pride, and oak's brown side,
　　Lord Richard's axe is ringing.

Up spoke the moody Elfin King,
　　Who wonn'd within the hill,—
Like wind in the porch of a ruin'd church,
　　His voice was ghostly shrill.

' Why sounds yon stroke on beech and oak,
　　Our moonlight circle's screen?
Or who comes here to chase the deer,
　　Beloved of our Elfin Queen?
Or who may dare on wold to wear
　　The fairies' fatal green?

' Up, Urgan, up! to yon mortal hie,
　　For thou wert christen'd man:
For cross or sign thou wilt not fly,
　　For mutter'd word or ban.

' Lay on him the curse of the wither'd heart,
　　The curse of the sleepless eye;
Till he wish and pray that his life would part,
　　Nor yet find leave to die!'

III

'Tis merry, 'tis merry, in good greenwood,
　　Though the birds have still'd their singing;
The evening blaze doth Alice raise,
　　And Richard is fagots bringing.

Up Urgan starts, that hideous dwarf,
  Before Lord Richard stands,
And as he cross'd and bless'd himself,
' I fear not sign,' quoth the grisly elf,
  ' That is made with bloody hands.'

But out then spoke she, Alice Brand,
  That woman void of fear,—
' And if there's blood upon his hand,
  'Tis but the blood of deer.'

—' Now loud thou liest, thou bold of mood!
  It cleaves unto his hand,
The stain of thine own kindly blood,
  The blood of Ethert Brand.'

Then forward stepp'd she, Alice Brand,
    And made the holy sign,—
' And if there's blood on Richard's hand,
    A spotless hand is mine.

' And I conjure thee, Demon elf,
    By Him whom Demons fear,
To show us whence thou art thyself,
    And what thine errand here ? '

IV

—' 'Tis merry, 'tis merry, in Fairy-land,
    When fairy birds are singing,
When the court doth ride by their monarch's side,
    With bit and bridle ringing :

' And gaily shines the Fairy-land—
    But all is glistening show,
Like the idle gleam that December's beam
    Can dart on ice and snow.

' And fading, like that varied gleam,
    Is our inconstant shape,
Who now like knight and lady seem,
    And now like dwarf and ape.

' It was between the night and day,
    When the Fairy King has power,
That I sunk down in a sinful fray,
And 'twixt life and death, was snatch'd away
    To the joyless Elfin bower.

' But wist I of a woman bold,
    Who thrice my brow durst sign,
I might regain my mortal mould,
    As fair a form as thine.'

'AND IF THERE'S BLOOD UPON HIS HAND,
'TIS BUT THE BLOOD OF DEER.'

She cross'd him once—she cross'd him twice—
　　That lady was so brave ;
The fouler grew his goblin hue,
　　The darker grew the cave.

She cross'd him thrice, that lady bold !
　　—He rose beneath her hand
The fairest knight on Scottish mould,
　　Her brother, Ethert Brand !

—Merry it is in good greenwood,
　　When the mavis and merle are singing ;
But merrier were they in Dumfermline gray
　　When all the bells were ringing.

Sir W. Scott.

O, WERT THOU IN THE CAULD BLAST

O, WERT thou in the cauld blast,
　　On yonder lea, on yonder lea,
My plaidie to the angry airt,
　　I'd shelter thee, I'd shelter thee.
Or did misfortune's bitter storms
　　Around thee blaw, around thee blaw,
Thy bield should be my bosom,
　　To share it a', to share it a'.

Or were I in the wildest waste
　　Of earth and air, of earth and air,
The desart were a paradise,
　　If thou wert there, if thou wert there.
Or were I monarch o' the globe,
　　Wi' thee to reign, wi' thee to reign,
The only jewel in my crown
　　Wad be my queen, wad be my queen.

R. Burns.

I LOVE MY JEAN

Of a' the airts the wind can blaw,
　I dearly like the west,
For there the bonie lassie lives,
　The lassie I lo'e best :
There wild woods grow, and rivers row,
　And monie a hill between ;
But day and night my fancy's flight
　Is ever wi' my Jean.

I see her in the dewy flowers,
　I see her sweet and fair ;
I hear her in the tunefu' birds,
　I hear her charm the air :
There's not a bonie flower that springs
　By fountain, shaw, or green ;
There's not a bonie bird that sings,
　But minds me o' my Jean.

R. Burns.

THERE'LL NEVER BE PEACE TILL JAMIE COMES HAME

A SONG

By yon castle wa', at the close of the day,
I heard a man sing, tho' his head it was grey:
And as he was singing, the tears fast down came—
There'll never be peace till Jamie comes hame.

The church is in ruins, the state is in jars,
Delusions, oppressions, and murderous wars;
We dare na weel say't but we ken wha's to blame—
There'll never be peace till Jamie comes hame.

My seven braw sons for Jamie drew sword,
And now I greet round their green beds in the yerd;
It brak the sweet heart o' my faithfu' auld dame—
There'll never be peace till Jamie comes hame.

Now life is a burden that bows me down,
Sin' I tint my bairns, and he tint his crown;
But till my last moment my words are the same—
There'll never be peace till Jamie comes hame.

R. BURNS.

THE BANKS O' DOON

YE flowery banks o' bonie Doon,
  How can ye blume sae fair!
How can ye chant, ye little birds,
  And I sae fu' o' care.

Thou'lt break my heart, thou bonie **bird**,
  That sings upon the bough;
Thou minds me o' the happy days,
  When my fause luve was true.

Thou'lt break my heart, thou bonie bird,
  That sings beside thy mate;
For sae I sat, and sae I sang,
  And wist na o' my fate.

Aft hae I rov'd by bonie Doon,
  To see the woodbine twine,
And ilka bird sang o' its love,
  And sae did I o' mine.

Wi' lightsome heart I pu'd a rose
  Frae off its thorny tree;
And my fause luver staw the rose,
  But left the thorn wi' me.

R. BURNS.

AS SLOW OUR SHIP

As slow our ship her foamy track
  Against the wind was cleaving,
Her trembling pennant still looked back
  To that dear isle 'twas leaving.

So loth we part from all we love,
  From all the links that bind us;
So turn our hearts, where'er we rove,
  To those we've left behind us!

F

When, round the bowl, of vanished years
   We talk, with joyous seeming,—
With smiles, that might as well be tears
   So faint, so sad their beaming;
While memory brings us back again
   Each early tie that twined us,
Oh, sweet's the cup that circles then
   To those we've left behind us!

And when, in other climes, we meet
   Some isle or vale enchanting,
Where all looks flowery, wild, and sweet,
   And nought but love is wanting;
We think how great had been our bliss,
   If Heaven had but assigned us
To live and die in scenes like this,
   With some we've left behind us!

As travellers oft look back, at eve,
   When eastward darkly going,
To gaze upon that light they leave
   Still faint behind them glowing,—
So, when the close of pleasure's day
   To gloom hath near consigned us,
We turn to catch one fading ray
   Of joy that's left behind us.

                         T. MOORE.

A RED, RED ROSE

O, MY luve's like a red, red rose,
   That's newly sprung in June:
O, my luve's like the melodie
   That's sweetly play'd in tune.

As fair art thou, my bonnie lass,
   So deep in luve am I:
And I will luve thee still, my dear,
   Till a' the seas gang dry.

Till a' the seas gang dry, my dear,
　And the rocks melt wi' the sun:
I will luve thee still, my dear,
　While the sands o' life shall run.

And fare thee weel, my only luve,
　And fare thee weel awhile !
And I will come again, my luve,
　Tho' it were ten thousand mile.

BANNOCKBURN

ROBERT BRUCE'S ADDRESS TO HIS ARMY

Scots, wha hae wi' Wallace bled,
Scots, wham Bruce has aften led ;
Welcome to your gory bed,
　Or to glorious victorie.

Now's the day, and now's the hour ;
See the front o' battle lower ;
See approach proud Edward's power—
　Edward ! chains and slaverie !

Wha will be a traitor knave ?
Wha can fill a coward's grave ?
Wha sae base as be a slave ?
　Traitor ! coward ! turn and flee !

Wha for Scotland's King and law
Freedom's sword will strongly draw,
Free-man stand, or free-man fa' ?
　Caledonian ! on wi' me !

By oppression's woes and pains !
By your sons in servile chains !
We will drain our dearest veins,
　But they shall—they *shall* be free !

Lay the proud usurpers low !
Tyrants fall in every foe !
Liberty's in every blow !
 Forward ! let us do, or die !

       R. Burns.

THE MINSTREL-BOY

The Minstrel-boy to the war is gone,
 In the ranks of death you'll find him ;
His father's sword he has girded on,
 And his wild harp slung behind him.—
' Land of song ! ' said the warrior-bard,
 ' Though all the world betrays thee,
One sword, at least, thy rights shall guard,
 One faithful harp shall praise thee ! '

The Minstrel fell !—but the foeman's chain
 Could not bring his proud soul under ;
The harp he loved ne'er spoke again,
 For he tore its chords asunder ;·
And said, ' No chains shall sully thee,
 Thou soul of love and bravery !
Thy songs were made for the brave and free,
 They shall never sound in slavery ! '

       T. Moore.

THE FAREWELL

It was a' for our rightfu' King,
 We left fair Scotland's strand ;
It was a' for our rightfu' King
 We e'er saw Irish land,
    My dear ;
We e'er saw Irish land.

Now a' is done that men can do,
And a' is done in vain ;
My love and native land farewell,
For I maun cross the main,
My dear ;
For I maun cross the main.

He turn'd him right and round about
    Upon the Irish shore;
And gae his bridle-reins a shake,
    With adieu for evermore,
            My dear;
    With adieu for evermore.

The sodger from the wars returns,
    The sailor frae the main;
But I hae parted frae my love,
    Never to meet again,
            My dear;
    Never to meet again.

When day is gane, and night is come,
    And a' folk bound to sleep;
I think on him that's far awa',
    The lee-lang night, and weep,
            My dear;
    The lee-lang night, and weep.

                      R. BURNS.

THE HARP THAT ONCE THROUGH TARA'S HALLS

THE harp that once through Tara's halls
    The soul of music shed,
Now hangs as mute on Tara's walls
    As if that soul were fled.
So sleeps the pride of former days,
    So glory's thrill is o'er,
And hearts, that once beat high for praise,
    Now feel that pulse no more.

No more to chiefs and ladies bright
    The harp of Tara swells:
The chord alone, that breaks at night,
    Its tale of ruin tells.

Thus Freedom now so seldom wakes,
 The only throb she gives
Is when some heart indignant breaks,
 To show that still she lives.

T. MOORE.

STANZAS

COULD Love for ever
Run like a river,
And Time's endeavour
 Be tried in vain—
No other pleasure
With this could measure;
And like a treasure
 We'd hug the chain.
But since our sighing
Ends not in dying,
And, form'd for flying,
 Love plumes his wing;

Then for this reason
 Let's love a season;
But let that season be only
 Spring.

When lovers parted
Feel broken-hearted,
And, all hopes thwarted
 Expect to die;
A few years older,
Ah! how much colder
They might behold her
 For whom they sigh!

LORD BYRON.

A SEA DIRGE

FULL fathom five thy father lies:
 Of his bones are coral made;
Those are pearls that were his eyes:
 Nothing of him that doth fade,
But doth suffer a sea-change
Into something rich and strange.
Sea-nymphs hourly ring his knell;
Hark! now I hear them—
 Ding, Dong, Bell.

W. SHAKESPEARE.

ROSE AYLMER

Ah! what avails the sceptred race,
   Ah! what the form divine!
What every virtue, every grace!
   Rose Aylmer, all were thine.

Rose Aylmer, whom these wakeful eyes
   May weep, but never see,
A night of memories and of sighs
   I consecrate to thee.

               W. S. LANDOR.

SONG

Who is Silvia ? what is she,
 That all our swains commend her ?
Holy, fair and wise is she ;
 The heaven such grace did lend her
That she might admired be.

Is she kind, as she is fair ?
 For beauty lives with kindness.
Love doth to her eyes repair,
 To help him of his blindness ;
And, being help'd, inhabits there.

Then to Silvia let us sing,
 That Silvia is excelling ;
She excels each mortal thing
 Upon the dull earth dwelling ;
To her let us garlands bring.

W. Shakespeare.

LUCY ASHTON'S SONG

Look not thou on beauty's charming,—
Sit thou still when kings are arming,—
Taste not when the wine-cup glistens,—
Speak not when the people listens,—
Stop thine ear against the singer,—
From the red gold keep thy finger,—
Vacant heart, and hand, and eye,
Easy live and quiet die.

Sir W. Scott.

EVENING

THE sun upon the lake is low,
  The wild birds hush their song;
The hills have evening's deepest glow,
  Yet Leonard tarries long.

Now all whom varied toil and care
  From home and love divide,
In the calm sunset may repair
  Each to the loved one's side.

ORPHEUS WITH HIS LUTE.

The noble dame on turret high,
  Who waits her gallant knight,
Looks to the western beam to spy
  The flash of armour bright.
The village maid, with hand on brow
  The level ray to shade,
Upon the footpath watches now
  For Colin's darkening plaid.

Now to their mates the wild swans row,
  By day they swam apart;
And to the thicket wanders slow
  The hind beside the hart.
The woodlark at his partner's side
  Twitters his closing song—
All meet whom day and care divide,—
  But Leonard tarries long !

Sir W. Scott

SONG

Orpheus with his lute made trees,
And the mountain tops that freeze,
  Bow themselves when he did sing :
To his music, plants and flowers
Ever sprung; as sun and showers
  There had made a lasting spring.

Everything that heard him play,
Even the billows of the sea,
  Hung their heads, and then lay by.
In sweet music is such art,
Killing care and grief of heart
  Fall asleep, or, hearing, die.

W. Shakespeare.

THE TWA CORBIES

As I was walking all alane,
I heard twa corbies making a mane;
The tane unto the t'other say,
'Whar sall we gang and dine the day?'

'In behint yon auld fail [1] dyke,
I wot there lies a new-slain knight;
And naebody kens that he lies there
But his hawk, his hound, and lady fair.

'His hound is to the hunting gane,
His hawk to fetch the wild-fowl hame,
His lady's ta'en another mate,
So we may make our dinner sweet.

'Ye'll sit on his white hause bane,
And I'll pike out his bonny blue e'en:
Wi' ae lock o' his gowden hair,
We'll theek our nest when it grows bare.

'Mony a one for him makes mane,
But nane sall ken whae he is gane:
O'er his white banes, when they are bare,
The wind sall blaw for evermair.'

[1] *Fail*, 'turf.'

TO ONE IN PARADISE

I

THOU wast all to me, love,
  For which my soul did pine—
A green isle in the sea, love,
  A fountain and a shrine,
All wreathed with fairy fruits and flowers,
  And all the flowers were mine.

II

Ah, dream, too bright to last!
  Ah, starry Hope! that didst arise
But to be overcast!
  A voice from out the Future cries,
'On! on!'—but o'er the Past
  (Dim gulf!) my spirit hovering lies
Mute, motionless, aghast!

III

For, alas! alas! with me
  The light of Life is o'er!
  'No more—no more—no more'—
(Such language holds the solemn sea
  To the sands upon the shore)
Shall bloom the thunder-blasted tree,
  Or the stricken eagle soar!

IV

And all my days are trances,
  And all my nightly dreams
Are where thy dark eye glances,
  And where thy footstep gleams;
In what ethereal dances,
  By what eternal streams.

E. A. POE.

HYMN TO DIANA

QUEEN and Huntress, chaste and fair,
    Now the sun is laid to sleep,
Seated in thy silver chair,
    State in wonted manner keep :
        Hesperus entreats thy light,
        Goddess excellently bright.

Earth, let not thy envious shade
 Dare itself to interpose ;
Cynthia's shining orb was made
  Heav'n to clear, when day did close :
   Bless us then with wishèd sight,
   Goddess excellently bright.

Lay thy bow of pearl apart
 And thy crystal shining quiver ;
Give unto the flying hart
  Space to breathe, how short soever :
   Thou that mak'st a day of night,
   Goddess excellently bright.

B. JONSON.

COUNTY GUY

AH ! County Guy, the hour is nigh,
 The sun has left the lea,
The orange flower perfumes the bower,
 The breeze is on the sea.
The lark, his lay who trill'd all day,
 Sits hush'd his partner nigh ;
Breeze, bird, and flower, confess the hour
 But where is County Guy ?

The village maid steals through the shade,
 Her shepherd's suit to hear ;
To beauty shy, by lattice high,
 Sings high-born Cavalier.
The star of Love, all stars above,
 Now reigns o'er earth and sky ;
And high and low the influence know—
 But where is County Guy ?

SIR W. SCOTT

G

GATHERING SONG OF DONALD DHU

PIBROCH of Donuil Dhu,
  Pibroch of Donuil,
Wake thy wild voice anew,
  Summon Clan Conuil.
Come away, come away,
  Hark to the summons !
Come in your war-array,
  Gentles and commons.

Come from deep glen, and
  From mountain so rocky,
The war-pipe and pennon
  Are at Inverlochy.
Come every hill-plaid, and
  True heart that wears one,
Come every steel blade, and
  Strong hand that bears one.

Leave untended the herd,
  The flock without shelter ;
Leave the corpse uninterr'd,
  The bride at the altar ;

Leave the deer, leave the steer,
  Leave nets and barges :
Come with your fighting gear,
  Broadswords and targes.

Come as the winds come, when
  Forests are rended ;
Come as the waves come, when
  Navies are stranded :
Faster come, faster come,
  Faster and faster,
Chief, vassal, page and groom,
  Tenant and master.

Fast they come, fast they come ;
  See how they gather !
Wide waves the eagle plume
  Blended with heather.
Cast your plaids, draw your
  blades,
  Forward each man set !
Pibroch of Donuil Dhu
  Knell for the onset !
                    SIR W. SCOTT.

THE DESTRUCTION OF SENNACHERIB

THE Assyrian came down like the wolf on the fold,
And his cohorts were gleaming in purple and gold ;
And the sheen of their spears was like stars on the sea,
When the blue wave rolls nightly on deep Galilee.

Like the leaves of the forest when Summer is green,
That host with their banners at sunset were seen ;
Like the leaves of the forest when Autumn hath blown,
That host on the morrow lay wither'd and strown.

AND THE IDOLS ARE BROKE IN THE TEMPLE OF BAAL.

For the Angel of Death spread his wings on the blast,
And breathed in the face of the foe as he pass'd ;
And the eyes of the sleepers wax'd deadly and chill,
And their hearts but once heaved, and for ever grew still !

And there lay the steed with his nostril all wide,
But through it there roll'd not the breath of his pride ;
And the foam of his gasping lay white on the turf,
And cold as the spray of the rock-beating surf.

And there lay the rider distorted and pale,
With the dew on his brow, and the rust on his mail :
And the tents were all silent, the banners alone,
The lances unlifted, the trumpet unblown.

And the widows of Ashur are loud in their wail,
And the idols are broke in the temple of Baal ;
And the might of the Gentile, unsmote by the sword,
Hath melted like snow in the glance of the Lord !

LORD BYRON.

THE CAVALIER

WHILE the dawn on the mountain was misty and gray,
My true love has mounted his steed, and away
Over hill, over valley, o'er dale, and o'er down,—
Heaven shield the brave Gallant that fights for the Crown !

He has doff'd the silk doublet the breastplate to bear,
He has placed the steel cap o'er his long-flowing hair,
From his belt to his stirrup his broadsword hangs down,—
Heaven shield the brave Gallant that fights for the Crown !

For the rights of fair England that broadsword he draws ;
Her King is his leader, her Church is his cause ;
His watchword is honour, his pay is renown,—
God strike with the Gallant that strikes for the Crown !

They may boast of their Fairfax, their Waller, and all
The roundheaded rebels of Westminster Hall;
But tell these bold traitors of London's proud town,
That the spears of the North have encircled the Crown.

There's Derby and Cavendish, dread of their foes;
There's Erin's high Ormond, and Scotland's Montrose!
Would you match the base Skippon, and Massey, and Brown
With the Barons of England, that fight for the Crown?

Now joy to the crest of the brave Cavalier!
Be his banner unconquer'd, resistless his spear,
Till in peace and in triumph his toils he may drown,
In a pledge to fair England, her Church, and her Crown.

Sir W. Scott.

ON FIRST LOOKING INTO CHAPMAN'S HOMER

Much have I travell'd in the realms of gold,
And many goodly states and kingdoms seen;
Round many western islands have I been
Which bards in fealty to Apollo hold.

Oft of one wide expanse had I been told
That deep-brow'd Homer ruled as his demesne:
Yet did I never breathe its pure serene
Till I heard Chapman speak out loud and bold:

Then felt I like some watcher of the skies
When a new planet swims into his ken;
Or like stout Cortez when with eagle eyes

He stared at the Pacific—and all his men
Look'd at each other with a wild surmise—
Silent, upon a peak in Darien.

J. Keats.

SONG

FOR MUSIC

A LAKE and a fairy boat
To sail in the moonlight clear,—
And merrily we would float
From the dragons that watch us here !

Thy gown should be snow-white silk,
And strings of orient pearls,
Like gossamers dipped in milk,
Should twine with thy raven curls

Red rubies should deck thy hands,
And diamonds should be thy dower—
But Fairies have broke their wands,
And wishing has lost its power !

T. HOOD.

ODE WRITTEN IN MDCCXLVI

How sleep the brave, who sink to rest,
By all their country's wishes bless'd!
When Spring, with dewy fingers cold,
Returns to deck their hallow'd mould,
She there shall dress a sweeter sod
Than Fancy's feet have ever trod.

By fairy hands their knell is rung;
By forms unseen their dirge is sung;
There Honour comes, a pilgrim gray,
To bless the turf that wraps their clay;
And Freedom shall a while repair
To dwell a weeping hermit there!

W. COLLINS.

TO DAFFODILS

FAIR Daffodils, we weep to see
    You haste away so soon:
As yet the early-rising Sun
    Has not attain'd his noon.

Stay, stay,
Until the hasting day
Has run
But to the even-song;
And, having pray'd together, we
Will go with you along.

We have short time to stay, as you,
 We have as short a Spring;
As quick a growth to meet decay,
 As you, or any thing.
  We die,
 As your hours do, and dry
  Away,
 Like to the Summer's rain;
Or as the pearls of morning's dew
 Ne'er to be found again.

R. Herrick.

THE SOLITARY REAPER

Behold her, single in the field,
Yon solitary Highland Lass!
Reaping and singing by herself;
Stop here, or gently pass!
Alone she cuts and binds the grain,
And sings a melancholy strain;
O listen! for the Vale profound
Is overflowing with the sound.

No Nightingale did ever chaunt
More welcome notes to weary bands
Of travellers in some shady haunt,
Among Arabian sands:
A voice so thrilling ne'er was heard
In spring-time from the Cuckoo-bird,
Breaking the silence of the seas
Among the farthest Hebrides.

Will no one tell me what she sings?—
Perhaps the plaintive numbers flow
For old, unhappy, far-off things,
And battles long ago:
Or is it some more humble lay,
Familiar matter of to-day?
Some natural sorrow, loss, or pain,
That has been, and may be again?

Whate'er the theme, the Maiden sang
As if her song could have no ending;
I saw her singing at her work,
And o'er the sickle bending;—

I listened, motionless and still;
And, as I mounted up the hill
The music in my heart I bore,
Long after it was heard no more.

W. WORDSWORTH.

TO BLOSSOMS

FAIR pledges of a fruitful tree,
　　Why do ye fall so fast ?
　　Your date is not so past ;
But you may stay yet here a while,
　　To blush and gently smile ;
　　　　And go at last.

What, were ye born to be
　　An hour or half's delight;
　　And so to bid good-night ?
'Twas pity Nature brought ye forth
　　Merely to show your worth,
　　　　And lose you quite.

But you are lovely leaves, where we
　　May read how soon things have
　　Their end, though ne'er so brave :
And after they have shown their pride,
　　Like you, a while : they glide
　　　　Into the grave.

R. HERRICK.

PROUD MAISIE

PROUD Maisie is in the wood,
　　Walking so early ;
Sweet Robin sits on the bush,
　　Singing so rarely.

' Tell me, thou bonny bird,
　　When shall I marry me ? '—
' When six braw gentlemen
　　Kirkward shall carry ye.'

' Who makes the bridal bed,
　　Birdie, say truly ? '—
' The grey-headed sexton
　　That delves the grave duly.

' The glow-worm o'er grave and stone
  Shall light thee steady.
The owl from the steeple sing,
  " Welcome, proud lady." '

SIR W. SCOTT.

SLEEP

Come, Sleep! O Sleep, the certain knot of peace,
  The baiting-place of wit, the balm of woe,
The poor man's wealth, the prisoner's release,
  Th' indifferent judge between the high and low;
With shield of proof shield me from out the press
  Of those fierce darts Despair at me doth throw:
O make in me those civil wars to cease;
  I will good tribute pay, if thou do so.
Take thou of me smooth pillows, sweetest bed,
  A chamber deaf of noise and blind of light,
A rosy garland and a weary head:
  And if these things, as being thine in right,
Move not thy heavy grace, thou shalt in me,
Livelier than elsewhere, Stella's image see.

SIR PHILIP SIDNEY.

HYMN FOR THE DEAD

That day of wrath, that dreadful day,
When heaven and earth shall pass away!
What power shall be the sinner's stay?
How shall he meet that dreadful day?

When, shrivelling like a parched scroll,
The flaming heavens together roll;
When louder yet, and yet more dread,
Swells the high trump that wakes the dead!

Oh! on that day, that wrathful day,
When man to judgment wakes from clay,
Be Thou the trembling sinner's stay,
Though heaven and earth shall pass away!

SIR W. SCOTT.

THE POPLAR FIELD

THE poplars are fell'd ; farewell to the shade,
And the whispering sound of the cool colonnade !
The winds play no longer and sing in the leaves,
Nor Ouse on his bosom their image receives.

Twelve years have elapsed since I last took a view
Of my favourite field, and the bank where they grew ;
And now in the grass behold they are laid,
And the tree is my seat that once lent me a shade !

The blackbird has fled to another retreat,
Where the hazels afford him a screen from the heat,
And the scene where his melody charm'd me before
Resounds with his sweet flowing ditty no more.

My fugitive years are all hasting away,
And I must ere long lie as lowly as they,
With a turf on my breast, and a stone at my head,
Ere another such grove shall arise in its stead.

'Tis a sight to engage me, if anything can,
To muse on the perishing pleasures of man ;
Short-lived as we are, our pleasures, I see
Have a still shorter date, and die sooner than we.

W. COWPER.

WINTER

WHEN icicles hang by the wall,
    And Dick the shepherd blows his nail,
And Tom bears logs into the hall,
    And milk comes frozen home in pail,
When blood is nipt, and ways be foul,
Then nightly sings the staring owl,
        Tuwhoo !
Tuwhit ! tuwhoo !   A merry note !
While greasy Joan doth keel the pot.

When all around the wind doth blow,
  And coughing drowns the parson's saw,
And birds sit brooding in the snow,
  And Marian's nose looks red and raw,
When roasted crabs hiss in the bowl,
Then nightly sings the staring owl
      Tuwhoo !
Tuwhit ! tuwhoo !   A merry note !
While greasy Joan doth keel the pot.

W. SHAKESPEARE.

ANNABEL LEE

IT was many and many a year ago,
  In a kingdom by the sea,
That a maiden there lived whom you may know
  By the name of Annabel Lee ;
And this maiden she lived with no other thought
  Than to love and be loved by me.

I was a child, and *she* was a child,
  In this kingdom by the sea ;
But we loved with a love that was more than love,
  I and my Annabel Lee ;
With a love that the wingèd seraphs of heaven
  Coveted her and me.

And this was the reason that, long ago,
  In this kingdom by the sea,
A wind blew out of a cloud, chilling
  My beautiful Annabel Lee ;
So that her high-born kinsmen came
  And bore her away from me,
To shut her up in a sepulchre
  In this kingdom by the sea.

TO SHUT HER UP IN A SEPULCHRE
IN THIS KINGDOM BY THE SEA.

H

The angels, not half so happy in heaven,
　　Went envying her and me ;
Yes !—that was the reason (as all men know,
　　In this kingdom by the sea)
That the wind came out of the cloud by night,
　　Chilling and killing my Annabel Lee.

But our love it was stronger by far than the love
　　Of those who were older than we—
　　Of many far wiser than we ;
And neither the angels in heaven above,
　　Nor the demons down under the sea,
Can ever dissever my soul from the soul
　　Of the beautiful Annabel Lee.

For the moon never beams, without bringing me dreams
    Of the beautiful Annabel Lee ;
And the stars never rise, but I see the bright eyes
    Of the beautiful Annabel Lee ;
And so, all the night-tide, I lie down by the side
Of my darling—my darling—my life and my bride,
    In her sepulchre there by the sea,
    In her tomb by the sounding sea.

                       E. A. POE.

TO MARY

IF I had thought thou couldst have died,
    I might not weep for thee ;
But I forgot, when by thy side,
    That thou couldst mortal be :
It never through my mind had past
    The time would e'er be o'er,
And I on thee should look my last,
    And thou shouldst smile no more !

And still upon that face I look,
    And think 'twill smile again ;
And still the thought I will not brook
    That I must look in vain !
But when I speak—thou dost not say
    What thou ne'er left'st unsaid ;
And now I feel, as well I may,
    Sweet Mary ! thou art dead.

If thou wouldst stay, e'en as thou art,
    All cold and all serene—
I still might press thy silent heart,
    And where thy smiles have been !
While e'en thy chill, bleak corse I have,
    Thou seemest still mine own ;
But there I lay thee in thy grave—
    And I am now alone !

I do not think, where'er thou art,
　　Thou hast forgotten me ;
And I, perhaps, may soothe this heart,
　　In thinking too of thee :
Yet there was round thee such a dawn
　　Of light ne'er seen before,
As fancy never could have drawn,
　　And never can restore !

C. WOLFE.

TWIST YE, TWINE YE

TWIST ye, twine ye ! even so,
Mingle shades of joy and woe,
Hope, and fear, and peace, and strife,
In the thread of human life.

While the mystic twist is spinning,
And the infant's life beginning,
Dimly seen through twilight bending,
Lo, what varied shapes attending !

Passions wild, and follies vain,
Pleasures soon exchanged for pain ;
Doubt, and jealousy, and fear,
In the magic dance appear.

Now they wax, and now they dwindle,
Whirling with the whirling spindle.
Twist ye, twine ye ! even so,
Mingle human bliss and woe.

SIR W. SCOTT.

TO LUCASTA, ON GOING TO THE WARS

TELL me not (sweet) I am unkind,
  That from the nunnery
Of thy chaste breast and quiet mind,
  To war and arms I fly.

True : a new mistress now I chase,
  The first foe in the field ;
And with a stronger faith embrace ·
  A sword, a horse, a shield.

Yet this inconstancy is such,
  As you too shall adore ;
I could not love thee, Dear, so much,
  Lov'd I not Honour more.

COLONEL LOVELACE.

THE DEMON LOVER

' O WHERE have you been, my long, long love,
  This long seven years and mair ? '
' O I'm come to seek my former vows
  Ye granted me before.'

' O hold your tongue of your former vows,
  For they will breed sad strife ;
O hold your tongue of your former vows,
  For I am become a wife.'

He turned him right and round about,
  And the tear blinded his e'e :
' I wad never hae trodden on Irish ground
  If it had not been for thee.

'I might hae had a king's daughter,
   Far, far beyond the sea;
I might have had a king's daughter,
   Had it not been for love o' thee.'

'If ye might have had a king's daughter,
   Yer sel ye had to blame;
Ye might have taken the king's daughter,
   For ye kend that I was nane.'

'O faulse are the vows o' womankind,
   But fair is their faulse bodie;
I never wad hae trodden on Irish ground,
   Had it not been for love o' thee.'

'If I was to leave my husband dear,
   And my two babes also,
O what have you to take me to,
   If with you I should go?'

'I hae seven ships upon the sea,
   The eighth brought me to land;
With four-and-twenty bold mariners,
   And music on every hand.'

She has taken up her two little babes,
   Kissed them baith cheek and chin;
'O fare ye weel, my ain twa babes,
   For I'll never see you again.'

She set her foot upon the ship,
   No mariners could she behold;
But the sails were o' the taffetie
   And the masts o' the beaten gold.

She had not sailed a league, a league,
   A league but barely three,
When dismal grew his countenance,
   And drumlie grew his e'e.

The masts, that were like the beaten gold,
   Bent not on the heaving seas;
But the sails, that were o' the taffetie,
   Fill'd not in the east land breeze.

They had not sailed a league, a league,
  A league but barely three,
Until she espied his cloven foot,
  And she wept right bitterlie.

' O hold your tongue of your weeping,' says he,
  ' Of your weeping now let me be ;
I will show you how the lilies grow
  On the banks of Italy.'

' O what hills are yon, yon pleasant hills,
  That the sun shines sweetly on ? '
' O yon are the hills of heaven,' he said,
  ' Where you will never win.'

' O whaten a mountain is yon, she said,
  ' All so dreary wi' frost and snow ? '
' O yon is the mountain of hell,' he cried,
  ' Where you and I will go.'

And aye when she turn'd her round about,
  Aye taller he seemed to be ;
Until that the tops o' the gallant ship
  Nae taller were than he.

The clouds grew dark, and the wind grew loud,
  And the leven filled her e'e ;
And waesome wail'd the snow-white sprites
  Upon the gurlie sea.

He strack the tapmast wi' his hand,
  The foremast wi' his knee ;
And he brake that gallant ship in twain,
  And sank her in the sea.

Minstrelsy of the Scottish Border.

THE LAWLANDS OF HOLLAND

THE Love that I have chosen
  I'll therewith be content;
The salt sea shall be frozen
  Before that I repent.
Repent it shall I never
  Until the day I dee!
But the Lawlands of Holland
  Have twinn'd my Love and me.

My Love he built a bonny ship,
  And set her to the main;
With twenty-four brave mariners
  To sail her out and hame.
But the weary wind began to rise,
  The sea began to rout,
And my Love and his bonny ship
  Turn'd withershins about.

There shall no mantle cross my back,
  No comb go in my hair,
Neither shall coal nor candle-light
  Shine in my bower mair;
Nor shall I choose another Love
  Until the day I dee,
Since the Lawlands of Holland
  Have twinn'd my Love and me.

' Now haud your tongue, my daughter dear,
  Be still, and bide content!
There's other lads in Galloway;
  Ye needna sair lament.'
—O there is none in Galloway,
  There's none at all for me :—
I never loved a lad but one,
  And he's drown'd in the sea.

                                  UNKNOWN.

THE VALLEY OF UNREST

Once it smiled a silent dell
Where the people did not dwell :
They had gone unto the wars,
Trusting to the mild-eyed stars,
Nightly from their azure towers
To keep watch above the flowers,
In the midst of which all day
The red sunlight lazily lay.
Now each visitor shall confess
The sad valley's restlessness.
Nothing there is motionless—
Nothing save the airs that brood
Over the magic solitude.
Ah, by no wind are stirred those trees
That palpitate like the chill seas
Around the misty Hebrides !
Ah, by no wind those clouds are driven
That rustle through the unquiet heaven
Unceasingly, from morn till even.
Over the violets there that lie
In myriad types of the human eye—
Over the lilies there that wave
And weep above a nameless grave !
They wave—from out their fragrant tops
Eternal dews come down in drops ;
They weep—from off their delicate stems
Perennial tears descend in gems.

E. A. POE.

THE BURIAL OF SIR JOHN MOORE AT CORUNNA

Not a drum was heard, not a funeral note,
 As his corse to the rampart we hurried ;
Not a soldier discharged his farewell shot
 O'er the grave where our hero we buried.

We buried him darkly at dead of night,
 The sods with our bayonets turning ;
By the struggling moonbeam's misty light,
 And the lantern dimly burning.

No useless coffin enclosed his breast,
 Not in sheet nor in shroud we wound him ;
But he lay like a warrior taking his rest,
 With his martial cloak around him.

Few and short were the prayers we said,
 And we spoke not a word of sorrow ;
But we steadfastly gazed on the face that was dead,
 And we bitterly thought of the morrow.

We thought, as we hollow'd his narrow bed,
 And smoothed down his lonely pillow,
That the foe and the stranger would tread o'er his head,
 And we far away on the billow !

Lightly they'll talk of the spirit that's gone,
 And o'er his cold ashes upbraid him,—
But little he'll reck, if they let him sleep on
 In the grave where a Briton has laid him.

But half of our heavy task was done
 When the clock struck the hour for retiring ;
And we heard the distant and random gun
 That the foe was sullenly firing.

Slowly and sadly we laid him down,
   From the field of his fame fresh and gory;
We carved not a line, and we raised not a stone—
   But we left him alone with his glory!

C. WOLFE.

ST. SWITHIN'S CHAIR

ON Hallow-Mass Eve, ere you boune ye to rest,
Ever beware that your couch be bless'd;
Sign it with cross, and sain it with bead,
Sing the Ave, and say the Creed.

For on Hallow-Mass Eve the Night-Hag will ride,
And all her nine-fold sweeping on by her side,
Whether the wind sing lowly or loud,
Sailing through moonshine or swath'd in the cloud.

The Lady she sate in St. Swithin's Chair,
The dew of the night has damp'd her hair:
Her cheek was pale—but resolved and high
Was the word of her lip and the glance of her eye.

She mutter'd the spell of Swithin bold,
When his naked foot traced the midnight wold,
When he stopp'd the Hag as she rode the night,
And bade her descend, and her promise plight.

He that dare sit on St. Swithin's Chair,
When the Night-Hag wings the troubled air,
Questions three, when he speaks the spell,
He may ask, and she must tell.

The Baron has been with King Robert his liege,
These three long years in battle and siege;
News are there none of his weal or his woe
And fain the Lady his fate would know.

She shudders and stops as the charm she speaks;—
Is it the moody owl that shrieks ?
Or is that sound, betwixt laughter and scream,
The voice of the Demon who haunts the stream ?

The moan of the wind sunk silent and low,
And the roaring torrent had ceased to flow ;
The calm was more dreadful than raging storm,
When the cold grey mist brought the ghastly form !

SIR W. SCOTT.

STANZAS WRITTEN ON THE ROAD BETWEEN FLORENCE AND PISA

OH, talk not to me of a name great in story;
The days of our youth are the days of our glory;
And the myrtle and ivy of sweet two-and-twenty
Are worth all your laurels, though ever so plenty.

What are garlands and crowns to the brow that is wrinkled?
'Tis but as a dead flower with May-dew besprinkled.
Then away with all such from the head that is hoary!
What care I for the wreaths that can *only* give glory!

Oh FAME!—if I e'er took delight in thy praises,
'Twas less for the sake of thy high-sounding phrases,
Than to see the bright eyes of the dear one discover,
She thought that I was not unworthy to love her.

There chiefly I sought thee, *there* only I found thee;
Her glance was the best of the rays that surround thee;
When it sparkled o'er aught that was bright in my story.
I knew it was love, and I felt it was glory.

LORD BYRON.

BARTHRAM'S DIRGE

THEY shot him dead on the Nine-Stone Rig,
  Beside the Headless Cross,
And they left him lying in his blood,
  Upon the moor and moss.

.   .   .   .   .   .

They made a bier of the broken bough,
  The sauch and the aspin gray,
And they bore him to the Lady Chapel,
  And waked him there all day.

A lady came to that lonely bower
  And threw her robes aside,
She tore her ling (long) yellow hair,
  And knelt at Barthram's side.

She bath'd him in the Lady-Well
  His wounds so deep and sair,
And she plaited a garland for his breast,
  And a garland for his hair.

They rowed him in a lily-sheet,
  And bare him to his earth,
(And the Grey Friars sung the dead man's mass,
  As they passed the Chapel Garth).

They buried him at (the mirk) midnight,
  (When the dew fell cold and still,
When the aspin gray forgot to play,
  And the mist clung to the hill).

They dug his grave but a bare foot deep,
  By the edge of the Nine-Stone Burn,
And they covered him (o'er with the heather-flower)
  The moss and the (Lady) fern.

A Grey Friar staid upon the grave,
  And sang till the morning tide,
And a friar shall sing for Barthram's soul,
  While Headless Cross shall bide.

R. SURTEES.

TO THE CUCKOO

  O BLITHE New-comer! I have heard,
    I hear thee and rejoice.
  O Cuckoo! shall I call thee Bird,
    Or but a wandering Voice?

  While I am lying on the grass
    Thy twofold shout I hear,
  From hill to hill it seems to pass,
    At once far off, and near.

Though babbling only to the Vale,
    Of sunshine and of flowers,
Thou bringest unto me a tale
    Of visionary hours.

Thrice welcome, darling of the Spring !
    Even yet thou art to me
No bird, but an invisible thing,
    A voice, a mystery ;

The same whom in my schoolboy days
   I listened to ; that Cry
Which made me look a thousand ways
   In bush, and tree, and sky.

To seek thee did I often rove
   Through woods and on the green ;
And thou wert still a hope, a love ;
   Still longed for, never seen.

And I can listen to thee yet ;
   Can lie upon the plain
And listen, till I do beget
   That golden time again.

O blessèd Bird ! the earth we pace
   Again appears to be
An unsubstantial, faery place :
   That is fit home for Thee !

W. WORDSWORTH.

HELEN OF KIRKCONNEL

I WISH I were where Helen lies !
Night and day on me she cries ;
O that I were where Helen lies,
   On fair Kirkconnel Lee !

Curst be the heart that thought the thought
And curst the hand, that fired the shot,
When in my arms burd Helen dropt,
   And died to succour me !

O think na ye my heart was sair,
When my love dropt down and spak' nae mair !
There did she swoon wi' meikle care,
   On fair Kirkconnel Lee.

As I went down the water side,
None but my foe to be my guide,
None but my foe to be my guide,
    On fair Kirkconnel Lee.

I lighted down, my sword did draw,
I hacked him into pieces sma',
I hacked him into pieces sma',
    For her sake that died for me.

O Helen fair, beyond compare !
I'll make a garland of thy hair,
Shall bind my heart for evermair,
    Untill the day I die.

O that I were where Helen lies !
Night and day on me she cries ;
Out of my bed she bids me rise,
    Says, 'Haste, and come to me !'

O Helen fair ! O Helen chaste !
If I were with thee, I were blest,
Where thou lies low, and takes thy rest,
    On fair Kirkconnel Lee.

I wish my grave were growing green,
A winding-sheet drawn ower my een,
And I in Helen's arms lying,
  On fair Kirkconnel Lee.

I wish I were where Helen lies!
Night and day on me she cries,
And I am weary of the skies,
  For her sake that died for me.

UNKNOWN.

TO ALTHEA FROM PRISON

WHEN Love with unconfinèd wings
  Hovers within my gates ;
And my divine Althea brings
  To whisper at the grates :
When I lie tangled in her hair,
  And fetter'd to her eye ;
The Gods that wanton in the air,
  Know no such liberty.

When flowing cups run swiftly round
  With no allaying Thames,
Our careless heads with roses bound,
  Our hearts with loyal flames ;
When thirsty grief in wine we steep,
  When healths and draughts go free,
Fishes that tipple in the deep,
  Know no such liberty.

When, like committed linnets, I
  With shriller throat shall sing
The sweetness, mercy, majesty,
  And glories of my KING ;
When I shall voice aloud, how good
  He is, how great should be ;
Enlargèd winds that curl the flood,
  Know no such liberty.

Stone walls do not a prison make,
    Nor iron bars a cage ;
Minds innocent and quiet take
    That for an hermitage ;

If I have freedom in my love,
  And in my soul am free;
Angels alone that soar above,
  Enjoy such liberty.

COLONEL LOVELACE.

' I WANDERED LONELY.'

I WANDERED lonely as a cloud
That floats on high o'er vales and hills,
When all at once I saw a crowd,
A host, of golden daffodils;
Beside the lake, beneath the trees,
Fluttering and dancing in the breeze.

Continuous as the stars that shine
And twinkle on the milky way,
They stretched in never-ending line
Along the margin of a bay:
Ten thousand saw I at a glance,
Tossing their heads in sprightly dance.

The waves beside them danced; but they
Out-did the sparkling waves in glee:
A poet could not but be gay,
In such a jocund company:
I gazed—and gazed—but little thought
What wealth the show to me had brought:

For oft, when on my couch I lie
In vacant or in pensive mood,
They flash upon that inward eye
Which is the bliss of solitude;
And then my heart with pleasure fills,
And dances with the daffodils.

W. WORDSWORTH.

HESTER

WHEN maidens such as Hester die,
Their place ye may not well supply,
Though ye among a thousand try,
  With vain endeavour.

A month or more hath she been dead,
Yet cannot I by force be led
To think upon the wormy bed
  And her together.

A springy motion in her gait,
A rising step, did indicate
Of pride and joy no common rate,
  That flushed her spirit.

I know not by what name beside
I shall it call:—if 'twas not pride,
It was a joy to that allied,
  She did inherit.

Her parents held the Quaker rule,
Which doth the human feeling cool,
But she was train'd in Nature's school,
    Nature had blest her.

A waking eye, a prying mind,
A heart that stirs, is hard to bind,
A hawk's keen sight ye cannot blind,
    Ye could not Hester.

My sprightly neighbour ! gone before
To that unknown and silent shore,
Shall we not meet, as heretofore,
    Some Summer morning,

When from thy cheerful eyes a ray
Hath struck a bliss upon the day,
A bliss that would not go away,
    A sweet fore-warning ?

C. LAMB.

TO EVENING

IF aught of oaten stop, or pastoral song,
May hope, chaste Eve, to soothe thy modest ear,
    Like thy own brawling springs,
    Thy springs, and dying gales ;

O Nymph reserved, while now the bright-hair'd sun
Sits in yon western tent, whose cloudy skirts,
    With brede ethereal wove,
    O'erhang his wavy bed :

Now air is hush'd, save where the weak-eyed bat
With short shrill shriek flits by on leathern wing,
    Or where the beetle winds
    His small but sullen horn,

As oft he rises midst the twilight path,
Against the pilgrim borne in heedless hum :—
    Now teach me, maid composed
    To breathe some soften'd strain,

Whose numbers, stealing through thy darkening vale,
May not unseemly with its stillness suit ;
    As, musing slow, I hail
    Thy genial loved return !

For when thy folding-star arising shows
His paly circlet, at his warning lamp
    The fragrant Hours, and Elves
    Who slept in buds the day,

And many a Nymph who wreathes her brows with sedge
And sheds the freshening dew, and, lovelier still,
    The pensive Pleasures sweet,
    Prepare thy shadowy car.

Then let me rove some wild and heathy scene ;
Or find some ruin midst its dreary dells,
    Whose walls more awful nod
    By thy religious gleams.

Or, if chill blustering winds, or driving rain
Prevent my willing feet, be mine the hut,
    That from the mountain's side,
    Views wilds, and swelling floods,

And hamlets brown, and dim-discover'd spires ;
And hears their simple bell, and marks o'er all
    Thy dewy fingers draw
    The gradual dusky veil.

While Spring shall pour his showers, as oft he wont,
And bathe thy breathing tresses, meekest Eve !
    While Summer loves to sport
    Beneath thy lingering light ;

While sallow Autumn fills thy lap with leaves ;
Or Winter, yelling through the troublous air,
    Affrights thy shrinking train,
    And rudely rends thy robes ;

So long, regardful of thy quiet rule,
Shall Fancy, Friendship, Science, smiling Peace,
    Thy gentlest influence own,
    And love thy favourite name !

                    W. COLLINS.

THE SUN UPON THE WEIRDLAW HILL

THE sun upon the Weirdlaw Hill,
    In Ettrick's vale, is sinking sweet ;
The westland wind is hush and still,
    The lake lies sleeping at my feet.
Yet not the landscape to mine eye
    Bears those bright hues that once it bore ;
Though evening, with her richest dye,
    Flames o'er the hills of Ettrick's shore.

With listless look along the plain,
    I see Tweed's silver current glide,
And coldly mark the holy fane
    Of Melrose rise in ruin'd pride.
The quiet lake, the balmy air,
    The hill, the stream, the tower, the tree,—
Are they still such as once they were?
    Or is the dreary change in me?

Alas, the warp'd and broken board,
    How can it bear the painter's dye!
The harp of strain'd and tuneless chord,
    How to the minstrel's skill reply!
To aching eyes each landscape lowers,
    To feverish pulse each gale blows chill;
And Araby's or Eden's bowers
    Were barren as this moorland hill.

Sir W. Scott

———————————————

THE WIFE OF USHER'S WELL

There lived a wife at Usher's Well,
    And a wealthy wife was she;
She had three stout and stalwart sons,
    And sent them o'er the sea.

They hadna been a week from her,
    A week but barely ane,
When word came to the carline wife,
    That her three sons were gane.

They had not been a week from her,
    A week but barely three,
When word came to the carline wife
    That her sons she'd never see.

' I wish the wind may never cease,
   Nor fishes in the flood,
Till my three sons come hame to me,
   In earthly flesh and blood ! '

It fell about the Martinmas,
   When nights are lang and mirk,
The carline wife's three sons came hame
   And their hats were o' the birk.

It neither grew in syke nor ditch,
   Nor yet in ony sheugh ;
But at the gates o' Paradise
   That birk grew fair eneugh.

' Blow up the fire, my maidens !
   Bring water from the well !
For a' my house shall feast this night,
   Since my three sons are well ! '

And she has made to them a bed,
   She's made it large and wide ;
And she's ta'en her mantle her about,
   Sat down at the bed-side.

Up then crew the red red cock,
   And up and crew the gray ;
The eldest to the youngest said,
   ' 'Tis time we were away ! '

The cock he hadna craw'd but once,
   And clapp'd his wings at a',
Whan the youngest to the eldest said,
   ' Brother, we must awa'.

' The cock doth craw, the day doth daw,
   The channerin' worm doth chide :
If we be miss'd out o' our place,
   A sair pain we maun bide.

'Fare ye well, my mother dear!
Farewell to barn and byre!
And fare ye weel, the bonny lass,
That kindles my mother's fire!'

UNKNOWN.

ALLEN-A-DALE

ALLEN-A-DALE has no fagot for burning,
Allen-a-Dale has no furrow for turning,
Allen-a-Dale has no fleece for the spinning,
Yet Allen-a-Dale has red gold for the winning.
Come, read me my riddle! come, hearken my tale!
And tell me the craft of bold Allen-a-Dale.

The Baron of Ravensworth prances in pride,
And he views his domains upon Arkindale side,
The mere for his net, and the land for his game,
The chase for the wild, and the park for the tame;
Yet the fish of the lake, and the deer of the vale,
Are less free to Lord Dacre than Allen-a-Dale!

Allen-a-Dale was ne'er belted a knight,
Though his spur be as sharp, and his blade be as bright:
Allen-a-Dale is no baron or lord,
Yet twenty tall yeomen will draw at his word;
And the best of our nobles his bonnet will vail,
Who at Rere-cross on Stanmore meets Allen-a-Dale.

Allen-a-Dale to his wooing is come;
The mother, she ask'd of his household and home:
'Though the castle of Richmond stand fair on the hill,
My hall,' quoth bold Allen, 'shows gallanter still;
'Tis the blue vault of heaven, with its crescent so pale,
And with all its bright spangles!' said Allen-a-Dale.

The father was steel, and the mother was stone;
They lifted the latch, and they bade him be gone;
But loud, on the morrow, their wail and their cry:
He had laugh'd on the lass with his bonny black eye.
And she fled to the forest to hear a love-tale,
And the youth it was told by was Allen-a-Dale!

SIR W. SCOTT.

THE BELEAGUERED CITY

I HAVE read, in some old marvellous tale,
  Some legend strange and vague,
That a midnight host of spectres pale
  Beleaguered the walls of Prague.

Beside the Moldau's rushing stream,
  With the wan moon overhead,
There stood, as in an awful dream,
  The army of the dead.

White as a sea-fog, landward bound,
  The spectral camp was seen,
And, with a sorrowful, deep sound,
  The river flowed between.

No other voice nor sound was there,
  No drum, nor sentry's pace;
The mist-like banners clasped the air,
  As clouds with clouds embrace.

But, when the old cathedral bell
  Proclaimed the morning prayer,
The white pavilions rose and fell
  On the alarmèd air.

Down the broad valley, fast and far
  The troubled army fled;
Up rose the glorious morning star,
  The ghastly host was dead.

I have read, in the marvellous heart of man,
  That strange and mystic scroll,
That an army of phantoms vast and wan
  Beleaguer the human soul.

Encamped beside Life's rushing stream,
  In Fancy's misty light,
Gigantic shapes and shadows gleam
  Portentous through the night.

Upon its midnight battle ground
  The spectral camp is seen,
And, with a sorrowful, deep sound,
  Flows the River of Life between.

No other voice, nor sound is there,
  In the army of the grave ;
No other challenge breaks the air,
  But the rushing of Life's wave.

And, when the solemn and deep church bell
  Entreats the soul to pray,
The midnight phantoms feel the spell,
  The shadows sweep away.

Down the broad Vale of Tears afar
  The spectral camp is fled ;
Faith shineth as a morning star,
  Our ghastly fears are dead.

                              H. W. LONGFELLOW.

ALEXANDER'S FEAST
OR, THE POWER OF MUSIC

'TWAS at the royal feast for Persia won
By Philip's warlike son—
Aloft in awful state
The godlike hero sate
On his imperial throne ;
His valiant peers were placed around,
Their brows with roses and with myrtles bound
(So should desert in arms be crown'd) ;

K

The lovely Thais by his side
Sate like a blooming eastern bride
In flower of youth and beauty's pride :—

Happy, happy, happy pair !
None but the brave
None but the brave
None but the brave deserves the fair !

   Timotheus placed on high
Amid the tuneful quire
With flying fingers touch'd the lyre :
The trembling notes ascend the sky
And heavenly joys inspire.
The song began from Jove
Who left his blissful seats above—
Such is the power of mighty love !
A dragon's fiery form belied the god ;
Sublime on radiant spires he rode
When he to fair Olympia prest,
And while he sought her snowy breast ;
Then round her slender waist he curl'd,
And stamp'd an image of himself, a sovereign of the
    world.
—The listening crowd admire the lofty sound !
A present deity ! they shout around :
A present deity ! the vaulted roofs rebound !
With ravish'd ears
The monarch hears,
Assumes the god,
Affects to nod
And seems to shake the spheres.

   The praise of Bacchus then the sweet musician sung—
Of Bacchus ever fair and ever young :
The jolly god in triumph comes !
Sound the trumpets, beat the drums !
Flush'd with a purple grace
He shows his honest face :
Now give the hautboys breath ; he comes, he comes !
Bacchus, ever fair and young,
Drinking joys did first ordain ;
Bacchus' blessings are a treasure,
Drinking is the soldier's pleasure :

Rich the treasure
Sweet the pleasure,
Sweet is pleasure after pain.

Soothed with the sound, the king grew vain;
Fought all his battles o'er again,
And thrice he routed all his foes, and thrice he slew the
    slain!
The master saw the madness rise,
His glowing cheeks, his ardent eyes;
And while he Heaven and Earth defied
Changed his hand and check'd his pride.
He chose a mournful Muse
Soft pity to infuse:
He sung Darius great and good,
By too severe a fate
Fallen, fallen, fallen, fallen,
Fallen from his high estate,
And weltering in his blood;
Deserted, at his utmost need,
By those his former bounty fed;
On the bare earth exposed he lies
With not a friend to close his eyes.
—With downcast looks the joyless victor sate,
Revolving in his alter'd soul
The various turns of Chance below;
And now and then a sigh he stole,
And tears began to flow.

The mighty master smiled to see
That love was in the next degree;
'Twas but a kindred sound to move,
For pity melts the mind to love.
Softly sweet, in Lydian measures
Soon he soothed his soul to pleasures.
War, he sung, is toil and trouble,
Honour but an empty bubble,
Never ending, still beginning;
Fighting still, and still destroying;
If the world be worth thy winning,
Think, O think, it worth enjoying:

Lovely Thais sits beside thee,
Take the good the gods provide thee!
—The many rend the skies with loud applause;
So Love was crown'd, but Music won the cause.
The prince, unable to conceal his pain,
Gazed on the fair
Who caused his care,
And sigh'd and look'd, sigh'd and look'd,
Sigh'd and look'd, and sigh'd again:
At length with love and wine at once opprest
The vanquish'd victor sunk upon her breast.

Now strike the golden lyre again:
A louder yet, and yet a louder strain!
Break his bands of sleep asunder
And rouse him like a rattling peal of thunder.
Hark, hark! the horrid sound
Has raised up his head:
As awaked from the dead
And amazed he stares around.
Revenge, revenge, Timotheus cries,
See the Furies arise!
See the snakes that they rear
How they hiss in their hair,
And the sparkles that flash from their eyes!
Behold a ghastly band
Each a torch in his hand!
Those are Grecian ghosts, that in battle were slain
And unburied remain
Inglorious on the plain:
Give the vengeance due
To the valiant crew!
Behold how they toss their torches on high,
How they point to the Persian abodes
And glittering temples of their hostile gods.
—The princes applaud with a furious joy:
And the King seized a flambeau with zeal to destroy;
Thais led the way
To light him to his prey,
And like another Helen, fired another Troy!

—Thus, long ago,
Ere heaving bellows learn'd to blow,
While organs yet were mute,
Timotheus, to his breathing flute

And sounding lyre
Could swell the soul to rage, or kindle soft desire.
At last divine Cecilia came,
Inventress of the vocal frame;

The sweet enthusiast from her sacred store
Enlarged the former narrow bounds,
And added length to solemn sounds,
With Nature's mother-wit, and arts unknown before.
—Let old Timotheus yield the prize
Or both divide the crown;
He raised a mortal to the skies;
She drew an angel down!

J. DRYDEN.

THE PASSIONATE SHEPHERD
TO HIS LOVE

Come live with me and be my love,
And we will all the pleasures prove
That hills and vallies, dales and fields,
And woods or steepy mountain yields.

And we will sit upon the rocks,
Seeing the shepherds feed their flocks
By shallow rivers to whose falls
Melodious birds sing madrigals.

And I will make thee beds of roses
And a thousand fragrant posies,
A cap of flowers, and a kirtle
Embroider'd all with leaves of myrtle.

A gown made of the finest wool,
Which from our pretty lambs we pull,
Fair-linèd slippers for the cold,
With buckles of the purest gold.

A belt of straw and ivy-buds
With coral clasps and amber studs,
An' if these pleasures may thee move,
Come live with me, and be my love.

Thy silver dishes for thy meat
As precious as the gods do eat,
Shall on an ivory table be
Prepar'd each day for thee and me.

The shepherd-swains shall dance and sing
For thy delight each May-morning:
If these delights thy mind may move,
Then live with me, and be my love.

C. Marlowe.

THE FLOWERS O' THE FOREST

I'VE heard them lilting, at the ewe-milking,
  Lasses a' lilting, before dawn o' day;
But now they are moaning, on ilka green loaning;
  The Flowers o' the Forest are a' wede awae.

At bughts, in the morning, nae blythe lads are scorning;
  Lasses are lonely, and dowie, and wae;
Nae daffing, nae gabbing, but sighing and sabbing;
  Ilk ane lifts her leglin, and hies her awae.

In har'st, at the shearing, nae youths now are jeering,
  Bandsters are lyart, and runkled, and gray;
At fair, or at preaching, nae wooing, nae fleeching;
  The Flowers o' the Forest are a' wede awae.

At e'en, in the gloaming, nae younkers are roaming
  'Bout stacks, wi' the lasses at bogles to play;
But ilk maid sits dreary, lamenting her dearie—
  The Flowers o' the Forest are weded awae.

Dool and wae for the order, sent our lads to the Border!
  The English, for ance, by guile wan the day;
The Flowers o' the Forest, that fought aye the foremost,
  The prime of our land, are cauld in the clay.

We'll hear nae mair lilting, at the ewe-milking;
  Women and bairns are heartless and wae:
Sighing and moaning, on ilka green loaning—
  The Flowers o' the Forest are a' wede awae.

E. ELLIOTT.

ULALUME

I

THE skies they were ashen and sober ;
　　The leaves they were crispèd and sere,—
　　The leaves they were withering and sere ;
It was night in the lonesome October
　　Of my most immemorial year ;
It was hard by the dim lake of Auber,
　　In the misty mid region of Weir,—
It was down by the dank tarn of Auber,
　　In the ghoul-haunted woodland of Weir.

II

Here once, through an alley Titanic
　　Of cypress, I roamed with my Soul,—
　　Of cypress, with Psyche, my Soul.
These were days when my heart was volcanic
　　As the scoriac rivers that roll,—
　　As the lavas that restlessly roll
Their sulphurous currents down Yaanek
　　In the ultimate climes of the pole,—
That groan as they roll down Mount Yaanek
　　In the realms of the boreal pole.

III

Our talk had been serious and sober,
　　But our thoughts they were palsied and sere,—
　　Our memories were treacherous and sere ;
For we knew not the month was October,
　　And we marked not the night of the year
　　(Ah, night of all nights in the year !)
We noted not the dim lake of Auber—
　　(Though once we had journeyed down here),
Remembered not the dank tarn of Auber,
　　Nor the ghoul-haunted woodland of Weir.

IV

And now, as the night was senescent,
 And star-dials pointed to morn,-
 As the sun-dials hinted of morn,
At the end of our path a liquescent
 And nebulous lustre was born,
Out of which a miraculous crescent
 Arose with a duplicate horn,—
Astartè's bediamonded crescent
 Distinct with its duplicate horn.

V

And I said, ' She is warmer than Dian :
 She rolls through an ether of sighs,—
 She revels in a region of sighs :
She has seen that the tears are not dry on
 'These cheeks, where the worm never dies,
And has come past the stars of the Lion :
 To point us the path to the skies—
 To the Lethean peace of the skies ;
Come up in despite of the Lion,
 To shine on us with her bright eyes ;
Come up through the lair of the Lion,
 With love in her luminous eyes.'

VI

But Psyche, uplifting her finger,
 Said—' Sadly, this star I mistrust—
 Her pallor I strangely mistrust—
Oh, hasten !—oh, let us not linger !
 Oh, fly !—let us fly !—for we must.'
In terror she spoke, letting sink her
 Wings until they trailed in the dust—
In agony sobbed, letting sink her
 Plumes till they trailed in the dust—
Till they sorrowfully trailed in the dust.

VII

I replied—' This is nothing but dreaming :
    Let us on by this tremulous light ;
    Let us bathe in this crystalline light :
Its sibyllic splendour is beaming
    With hope and in beauty to-night :—
    See !—it flickers up the sky through the night ;

Ah, we safely may trust to its gleaming,
    And be sure it will lead us aright—
We safely may trust to a gleaming
    That cannot but guide us aright,
    Since it flickers up to Heaven through the night.'

VIII

Thus I pacified Psyche and kissed her,
    And tempted her out of her gloom—
    And conquered her scruples and gloom;
And we passed to the end of a vista,
    But were stopped by the door of a tomb—
    By the door of a legended tomb;
And I said, ' What is written, sweet sister,
    On the door of this legended tomb ? '
    She replied :—' Ulalume—Ulalume—
    'Tis the vault of thy lost Ulalume ! '

IX

Then my heart it grew ashen and sober
    As the leaves that were crisped and sere,
    As the leaves that were withering and sere;
And I cried—' It was surely October
    On *this* very night of last year,
    That I journeyed—I journeyed down here—
    That I brought a dread burden down here !
    On this night of all nights in the year;
    Ah, what demon has tempted me here ?
    Well I know, now, this dim lake of Auber—
        This misty mid region of Weir—
    Well I know, now, this dank tarn of Auber,—
        This ghoul-haunted woodland of Weir.'

                      E. A. POE.

KUBLA KHAN

In Xanadu did Kubla Khan
A stately pleasure-dome decree:
Where Alph, the sacred river, ran
Through caverns measureless to man
    Down to a sunless sea.
So twice five miles of fertile ground
With walls and towers were girdled round:
And there were gardens bright with sinuous rills
Where blossom'd many an incense-bearing tree;
And here were forests ancient as the hills,
Enfolding sunny spots of greenery.

But oh! that deep romantic chasm which slanted
Down the green hill athwart a cedarn cover!
A savage place! as holy and enchanted
As e'er beneath a waning moon was haunted
By woman wailing for her demon-lover!
And from this chasm, with ceaseless turmoil seething
As if this earth in fast thick pants were breathing,
A mighty fountain momently was forced:
Amid whose swift half-intermitted burst
Huge fragments vaulted like rebounding hail,
Or chaffy grain beneath the thresher's flail;
And 'mid these dancing rocks at once and ever
It flung up momently the sacred river.
Five miles meandering with a mazy motion
Through wood and dale the sacred river ran,
Then reach'd the caverns measureless to man,
And sank in tumult to a lifeless ocean:
And 'mid this tumult Kubla heard from far
Ancestral voices prophesying war!

The shadow of the dome of pleasure
Floated midway on the waves;
Where was heard the mingled measure
From the fountain and the caves.

It was a miracle of rare device,
A sunny pleasure-dome with caves of ice!
A damsel with a dulcimer
In a vision once I saw:
It was an Abyssinian maid,
And on her dulcimer she played,

Singing of Mount Abora.
Could I revive within me
Her symphony and song,
 To such a deep delight 'twould win me
That with music loud and long,
I would build that dome in air,
That sunny dome! Those caves of ice!
And all who heard should see them there
And all should cry, Beware! Beware!
His flashing eyes, his floating hair!
Weave a circle round him thrice,
And close your eyes with holy dread
For he on honey-dew hath fed,
And drunk the milk of Paradise.

S. T. COLERIDGE.

L'ALLEGRO

HENCE, loathèd Melancholy,
 Of Cerberus and blackest Midnight born
In Stygian cave forlorn
 'Mongst horrid shapes, and shrieks, and sights unholy!
Find out some uncouth cell
 Where brooding Darkness spreads his jealous wings
 And the night-raven sings;
  There under ebon shades, and low-brow'd rocks
 As ragged as thy locks,
  In dark Cimmerian desert ever dwell.

 But come, thou Goddess fair and free,
In heaven yclept Euphrosynè,
And by men, heart-easing Mirth,
Whom lovely Venus at a birth
With two sister Graces more
To ivy-crownèd Bacchus bore:
Or whether (as some sager sing)
The frolic wind that breathes the spring

Zephyr, with Aurora playing,
As he met her once a-Maying—
There on beds of violets blue
And fresh-blown roses wash'd in dew

Fill'd her with thee, a daughter fair,
So buxom, blithe, and debonair.
  Haste thee, Nymph, and bring with thee
Jest, and youthful jollity,

L

Quips, and cranks, and wanton wiles,
Nods, and becks, and wreathèd smiles
Such as hang on Hebe's cheek,
And love to live in dimple sleek;
Sport that wrinkled Care derides,
And Laughter holding both his sides:—
Come, and trip it as you go
On the light fantastic toe;
And in thy right hand lead with thee
The mountain nymph, sweet Liberty;
And if I give thee honour due,
Mirth, admit me of thy crew,
To live with her, and live with thee
In unreprovèd pleasures free;
To hear the lark begin his flight
And singing startle the dull night
From his watch-tower in the skies,
Till the dappled dawn doth rise;
Then to come, in spite of sorrow,
And at my window bid good-morrow
Through the sweetbriar, or the vine,
Or the twisted eglantine:
While the cock with lively din
Scatters the rear of darkness thin,
And to the stack, or the barn-door,
Stoutly struts his dames before:
Oft listening how the hounds and horn
Cheerly rouse the slumbering morn:
From the side of some hoar hill,
Through the high wood echoing shrill.
Sometime walking, not unseen,
By hedge-row elms, on hillocks green,
Right against the eastern gate
Where the great Sun begins his state
Robed in flames and amber light;
The clouds in thousand liveries dight;
While the ploughman, near at hand,
Whistles o'er the furrow'd land,
And the milkmaid singeth blithe,
And the mower whets his scythe,

And every shepherd tells his tale
Under the hawthorn in the dale.

   Straight mine eye hath caught new pleasures
Whilst the landscape round it measures;
Russet lawns, and fallows gray,
Where the nibbling flocks do stray;
Mountains, on whose barren breast
The labouring clouds do often rest;
Meadows trim with daisies pied,
Shallow brooks, and rivers wide;
Towers and battlements it sees
Bosom'd high in tufted trees,
Where perhaps some Beauty lies,
The Cynosure of neighbouring eyes.

   Hard by, a cottage chimney smokes
From betwixt two agèd oaks,
Where Corydon and Thyrsis, met,
Are at their savoury dinner set
Of herbs, and other country messes
Which the neat-handed Phillis dresses;
And then in haste her bower she leaves
With Thestylis to bind the sheaves;
Or, if the earlier season lead,
To the tann'd haycock in the mead.

   Sometimes with secure delight
The upland hamlets will invite,
When the merry bells ring round,
And the jocund rebecks sound
To many a youth and many a maid,
Dancing in the chequer'd shade;
And young and old come forth to play
On a sunshine holy-day,
Till the live-long daylight fail:
Then to the spicy nut-brown ale,
With stories told of many a feat,
How faery Mab the junkets eat;
She was pinch'd, and pull'd, she said;
And he, by friar's lantern led;
Tells how the drudging Goblin sweat
To earn his cream-bowl duly set,

When in one night, ere glimpse of morn,
His shadowy flail hath thresh'd the corn
That ten day-labourers could not end;
Then lies him down the lubber fiend,
And, stretch'd out all the chimney's length,
Basks at the fire his hairy strength;

And crop-full out of doors he flings,
Ere the first cock his matin rings.

Thus done the tales, to bed they creep,
By whispering winds soon lulled asleep.

Tower'd cities please us then
And the busy hum of men,
Where throngs of knights and barons bold,
In weeds of peace high triumphs hold,
With store of ladies, whose bright eyes
Rain influence, and judge the prize
Of wit or arms, while both contend
To win her grace, whom all commend.
There let Hymen oft appear
In saffron robe, with taper clear,
And pomp, and feast, and revelry,
With mask, and antique pageantry;
Such sights as youthful poets dream
On summer eves by haunted stream.
Then to the well-trod stage anon,
If Jonson's learned sock be on,
Or sweetest Shakespeare, Fancy's child,
Warble his native wood-notes wild.

And ever against eating cares
Lap me in soft Lydian airs
Married to immortal verse,
Such as the meeting soul may pierce
In notes, with many a winding bout
Of linkèd sweetness long drawn out;
With wanton heed and giddy cunning,
The melting voice through mazes running,
Untwisting all the chains that tie
The hidden soul of harmony;
That Orpheus' self may heave his head
From golden slumber, on a bed
Of heap'd Elysian flowers, and hear
Such strains as would have won the ear
Of Pluto, to have quite set free
His half-regain'd Eurydicè.

These delights if thou canst give,
Mirth, with thee I mean to live.

J. MILTON

IL PENSEROSO

HENCE, vain deluding Joys,
   The brood of Folly without father bred!
How little you bestead
   Or fill the fixèd mind with all your toys!
Dwell in some idle brain,
   And fancies fond with gaudy shapes possess
As thick and numberless
   As the gay motes that people the sunbeams,
Or likest hovering dreams
   The fickle pensioners of Morpheus' train.

   But hail, thou goddess sage and holy,
Hail, divinest Melancholy!
Whose saintly visage is too bright
To hit the sense of human sight,
And therefore to our weaker view
O'erlaid with black, staid Wisdom's hue;
Black, but such as in esteem
Prince Memnon's sister might beseem,
Or that starr'd Ethiop queen that strove
To set her beauty's praise above
The sea nymphs, and their powers offended
Yet thou art higher far descended:
Thee bright-haired Vesta, long of yore,
To solitary Saturn bore;
His daughter she; in Saturn's reign
Such mixture was not held a stain:
Oft in glimmering bowers and glades
He met her, and in secret shades
Of woody Ida's inmost grove,
While yet there was no fear of Jove.
   Come, pensive nun, devout and pure,
Sober, steadfast, and demure,
All in a robe of darkest grain
Flowing with majestic train,
And sable stole of cypress lawn
Over thy decent shoulders drawn:

Come, but keep thy wonted state,
With even step, and musing gait,
And looks commercing with the skies,
Thy rapt soul sitting in thine eyes :
There, held in holy passion still,
Forget thyself to marble, till,
With a sad leaden downward cast,
Thou fix them on the earth as fast ;
And join with thee, calm Peace, and Quiet
Spare Fast, that oft with gods doth diet,
And hears the Muses in a ring
Aye round about Jove's altar sing :
And add to these retired Leisure,
That in trim gardens takes his pleasure :—
But first, and chiefest, with thee bring
Him that yon soars on golden wing,
Guiding the fiery-wheelèd throne,
The cherub Contemplatiòn ;
And the mute Silence hist along,
'Less Philomel will deign a song
In her sweetest, saddest plight,
Smoothing the rugged brow of Night.
While Cynthia checks her dragon yoke
Gently o'er the accustom'd oak.
—Sweet bird, that shunn'st the noise of folly,
Most musical, most melancholy !
Thee, chauntress, oft, the woods among
I woo, to hear thy even-song ;
And missing thee, I walk unseen
On the dry, smooth-shaven green,
To behold the wandering Moon
Riding near her highest noon,
Like one that had been led astray
Through the heaven's wide pathless way
And oft, as if her head she bow'd,
Stooping through a fleecy cloud.
    Oft, on a plat of rising ground
I hear the far-off curfeu sound
Over some wide-water'd shore,
Swinging slow with sullen roar :

Or, if the air will not permit,
Some still removèd place will fit,
Where glowing embers through the room
Teach light to counterfeit a gloom ;
Far from all resort of mirth,
Save the cricket on the hearth,

Or the bellman's drowsy charm
To bless the doors from nightly harm.
  Or let my lamp at midnight hour
Be seen in some high lonely tower,
Where I may oft out-watch the Bear
With thrice-great Hermes, or unsphere
The spirit of Plato, to unfold
What worlds or what vast regions hold
The immortal mind, that hath forsook
Her mansion in this fleshly nook.
And of those demons that are found
In fire, air, flood, or under ground,
Whose power hath a true consent
With planet, or with element.
Sometime let gorgeous Tragedy
In scepter'd pall come sweeping by,
Presenting Thebes, or Pelops' line,
Or the tale of Troy divine;
Or what (though rare) of later age
Ennobled hath the buskin'd stage.
  But, O sad Virgin, that thy power
Might raise Musaeus from his bower,
Or bid the soul of Orpheus sing
Such notes as, warbled to the string,
Drew iron tears down Pluto's cheek
And made Hell grant what Love did seek,
Or call up him that left half-told
The story of Cambuscan bold,
Of Camball, and of Algarsife,
And who had Canacè to wife
That own'd the virtuous ring and glass;
And of the wondrous horse of brass
On which the Tartar king did ride:
And if aught else great bards beside
In sage and solemn tunes have sung
Of turneys, and of trophies hung,
Of forests, and enchantments drear,
Where more is meant than meets the ear.
  Thus, Night, oft see me in thy pale career,
Till civil-suited Morn appear

Not trick'd and frounced as she was wont
With the Attic Boy to hunt,
But kercheft in a comely cloud
While rocking winds are piping loud,
Or usher'd with a shower still,
When the gust hath blown his fill,
Ending on the rustling leaves
With minute-drops from off the eaves.

And when the sun begins to fling
His flaring beams, me, Goddess bring
To archèd walks of twilight groves,
And shadows brown, that Sylvan loves,
Of pine, or monumental oak,
Where the rude axe, with heavèd stroke,
Was never heard the nymphs to daunt
Or fright them from their hallow'd haunt.

There in close covert by some brook
Where no profaner eye may look,
Hide me from day's garish eye,
While the bee with honey'd thigh
That at her flowery work doth sing,
And the waters murmuring,
With such concert as they keep,
Entice the dewy-feather'd Sleep;
And let some strange mysterious dream
Wave at his wings in aery stream
Of lively portraiture display'd,
Softly on my eyelids laid:
And, as I wake, sweet music breathe
Above, about, or underneath,
Sent by some spirit to mortals good,
Or the unseen Genius of the wood.

But let my due feet never fail
To walk the studious cloister's pale,
And love the high-embowèd roof,
With antique pillars massy proof,
And storied windows richly dight,
Casting a dim religious light:
There let the pealing organ blow
To the full-voiced quire below
In service high and anthems clear,
As may with sweetness, through mine ear,
Dissolve me into ecstasies,
And bring all Heaven before mine eyes.

And may at last my weary age
Find out the peaceful hermitage,
The hairy gown and mossy cell,
Where I may sit and rightly spell
Of every star that heaven doth show,
And every herb that sips the dew;
Till old experience do attain
To something like prophetic strain.

These pleasures, Melancholy, give,
And I with thee will choose to live.

J. MILTON.

JOCK OF HAZELDEAN

I

' WHY weep ye by the tide, ladie ?
　Why weep ye by the tide ?
I'll wed ye to my youngest son,
　And ye sall be his bride :
And ye sall be his bride, ladie,
　Sae comely to be seen '—
But aye she loot the tears down fa'
　For Jock of Hazeldean.

II

' Now let this wilfu' grief be done,
　And dry that cheek so pale ;
Young Frank is chief of Errington,
　And lord of Langley-dale ;
His step is first in peaceful ha',
　His sword in battle keen '—
But aye she loot the tears down fa'
　For Jock of Hazeldean.

III

' A chain of gold ye sall not lack,
　Nor braid to bind your hair ;
Nor mettled hound, nor managed hawk,
　Nor palfrey fresh and fair ;
And you, the foremost o' them a',
　Shall ride our forest queen '—
But aye she loot the tears down fa'
　For Jock of Hazeldean.

'WHY WEEP YE BY THE TIDE, LADIE?'

IV

The kirk was deck'd at morning-tide,
   The tapers glimmer'd fair ;
The priest and bridegroom wait the bride,
   And dame and knight are there.
They sought her baith by bower and ha'
   The ladie was not seen !
She's o'er the Border, and awa'
   Wi' Jock of Hazeldean.

SIR W. SCOTT.

THE RECOLLECTION

WE wander'd to the pine forest
   That skirts the ocean's foam ;
The lightest wind was in its nest,
   The tempest in its home.
The whispering waves were half asleep,
   The clouds were gone to play,
And on the bosom of the deep
   The smile of heaven lay ;
It seem'd as if the hour were one
   Sent from beyond the skies,
Which scatter'd from above the sun
   A light of paradise !

We paused amid the pines that stood
   The giants of the waste,
Tortured by storms to shapes as rude
   As serpents interlaced,
And soothed, by every azure breath
   That under heaven is blown,
To harmonies and hues beneath,
   As tender as its own ;
Now all the tree-tops lay asleep
   Like green waves on the sea,
As still as in the silent deep
   The ocean woods may be.

How calm it was !—the silence there
  By such a chain was bound
That even the busy woodpecker
  Made stiller by her sound
The inviolable quietness ;
  The breath of peace we drew
With its soft motion made not less
  The calm that round us grew.
There seemed, from the remotest seat
  Of the white mountain waste
To the soft flower beneath our feet,
  A magic circle traced,—
A spirit interfused around,
  A thrilling silent life :
To momentary peace it bound
  Our mortal nature's strife.
And still, I felt, the centre of
  The magic circle there
Was one fair form that fill'd with love
  The lifeless atmosphere.

We paused beside the pools that lie
  Under the forest bough.
Each seem'd as 'twere a little sky
  Gulf'd in a world below :
A firmament of purple light
  Which in the dark earth lay,
More boundless than the depth of night
  And purer than the day—
In which the lovely forests grew
  As in the upper air,
More perfect both in shape and hue
  Than any spreading there.
There lay the glade, the neighbouring lawn,
  And through the dark-green wood
The white sun twinkling like the dawn
  Out of a speckled cloud.
Sweet views which in our world above
  Can never well be seen
Were imaged by the water's love
  Of that fair forest green ;

And all was interfused beneath
   With an Elysian glow,
An atmosphere without a breath,
   A softer day below.

Like one beloved, the scene had lent
   To the dark water's breast
Its every leaf and lineament
   With more than truth exprest;
Until an envious wind crept by,—
   Like an unwelcome thought
Which from the mind's too faithful eye
   Blots one dear image out.
Though Thou art ever fair and kind,
   And forests ever green,
Less oft is peace in Shelley's mind
   Than calm in waters seen.

P. B. SHELLEY.

AULD ROBIN GRAY

WHEN the sheep are in the fauld, and the kye at hame,
And a' the warld to rest are gane,
The waes o' my heart fa' in showers frae my e'e,
While my gudeman lies sound by me.

Young Jamie lo'ed me weel, and sought me for his bride;
But saving a croun he had naething else beside:
To make the croun a pund, young Jamie gaed to sea;
And the croun and the pund were baith for me.

He hadna been awa' a week but only twa,
When my father brak his arm, and the cow was stown awa';
My mother she fell sick, and my Jamie at the sea—
And auld Robin Gray came a-courtin' me.

My father couldna work, and my mother couldna spin;
I toil'd day and night, but their bread I couldna win;
Auld Rob maintain'd them baith, and wi' tears in his e'e
Said, 'Jennie, for their sakes, O, marry me!'

M

My heart it said nay; I look'd for Jamie back;
But the wind it blew high, and the ship it was a wrack
His ship it was a wrack—why didna Jamie dee,
Or why do I live to cry, Wae's me?

My father urgit sair: my mother didna speak;
But she look'd in my face till my heart was like to break:
They gi'ed him my hand, but my heart was at the sea:
Sae auld Robin Gray he was gudeman to me.

I hadna been a wife a week but only four,
When mournfu' as I sat on the stane at the door,
I saw my Jamie's wraith, for I couldna think it he—
Till he said, 'I'm come hame to marry thee.'

—O sair, sair did we greet, and muckle did we say;
We took but ae kiss, and I bad him gang away:
I wish that I were dead, but I'm no like to dee;
And why was I born to say, Wae's me!

I gang like a ghaist, and I carena to spin;
I daurna think on Jamie, for that wad be a sin;
But I'll do my best a gude wife aye to be,
For auld Robin Gray he is kind unto me.

LADY A. LINDSAY.

WILLIE DROWNED IN YARROW

Down in yon garden sweet and gay
  Where bonnie grows the lily,
I heard a fair maid sighing say,
  ' My wish be wi' sweet Willie !

' Willie's rare, and Willie's fair,
  And Willie's wondrous bonny;
And Willie hecht to marry me
  Gin e'er he married ony.

' O gentle wind, that bloweth south,
  From where my Love repaireth,
Convey a kiss frae his dear mouth
  And tell me how he fareth !

' O tell sweet Willie to come doun
  And hear the mavis singing,
And see the birds on ilka bush
  And leaves around them hinging

' The lav'rock there, wi' her white breast
  And gentle throat sae narrow :
There's sport eneuch for gentlemen
  On Leader-haughs and Yarrow.

' O Leader-haughs are wide and braid
  And Yarrow-haughs are bonny ;
There Willie hecht to marry me
  If e'er he married ony.

' But Willie's gone, whom I thought on,
  And does not hear me weeping ;
Draws many a tear frae true love's e'e
  When other maids are sleeping.

' O came ye by yon water-side ?
  Pou'd you the rose or lily ?
Or came you by yon meadow green,
  Or saw you my sweet Willie ? '

She sought him up, she sought him down,
  She sought him braid and narrow ;
Syne, in the cleaving of a craig,
  She found him drown'd in Yarrow !

UNKNOWN.

THE REVERIE OF POOR SUSAN

AT the corner of Wood Street, when daylight appears,
Hangs a Thrush that sings loud, it has sung for three years :
Poor Susan has passed by the spot, and has heard
In the silence of morning the song of the Bird.

'Tis a note of enchantment ; what ails her ?   She sees
A mountain ascending, a vision of trees ;
Bright volumes of vapour through Lothbury glide,
And a river flows on through the vale of Cheapside.

Green pastures she views in the midst of the dale,
Down which she so often has tripped with her pail ;
And a single small cottage, a nest like a dove's,
The one only dwelling on earth that she loves.

SYNE, IN THE CLEAVING OF A CRAIG.

She looks, and her heart is in heaven: but they fade.
The mist and the river, the hill and the shade:
The stream will not flow, and the hill will not rise,
And the colours have all passed away from her eyes!

W. WORDSWORTH.

THE ARMADA

A FRAGMENT

ATTEND, all ye who list to hear our noble England's praise;
I tell of the thrice famous deeds she wrought in ancient days,
When that great fleet invincible against her bore in vain
The richest spoils of Mexico, the stoutest hearts of Spain.

It was about the lovely close of a warm summer day,
There came a gallant merchant-ship full sail to Plymouth Bay;
Her crew hath seen Castile's black fleet, beyond Aurigny's isle,
At earliest twilight, on the waves lie heaving many a mile.
At sunrise she escaped their van, by God's especial grace;
And the tall 'Pinta,' till the noon, had held her close in chase.
Forthwith a guard at every gun was placed along the wall;
The beacon blazed upon the roof of Edgecumbe's lofty hall;
Many a light fishing-bark put out to pry along the coast,
And with loose rein and bloody spur rode inland many a post.
With his white hair unbonneted, the stout old sheriff comes;
Behind him march the halberdiers; before him sound the drums;
His yeomen round the market cross make clear an ample space;
For there behoves him to set up the standard of Her Grace.
And haughtily the trumpets peal, and gaily dance the bells
As slow upon the labouring wind the royal blazon swells.
Look how the Lion of the sea lifts up his ancient crown,
And underneath his deadly paw treads the gay lilies down.
So stalked he when he turned to flight, on that famed Picard
    field,
Bohemia's plume, and Genoa's bow, and Cæsar's eagle shield.
So glared he when at Agincourt in wrath he turned to bay,
And crushed and torn beneath his claws the princely hunters lay.

Ho! strike the flagstaff deep, Sir Knight : ho ! scatter flowers, fair
    maids :
Ho ! gunners, fire a loud salute : ho ! gallants, draw your blades :
Thou sun, shine on her joyously ; ye breezes, waft her wide ;
Our glorious SEMPER EADEM, the banner of our pride.

    The freshening breeze of eve unfurled that banner's massy fold ;
The parting gleam of sunshine kissed that haughty scroll of gold ;
Night sank upon the dusky beach, and on the purple sea,
Such night in England ne'er had been, nor e'er again shall be.

From Eddystone to Berwick bounds, from Lynn to Milford Bay,
That time of slumber was as bright and busy as the day;
For swift to east and swift to west the ghastly war-flame spread,
High on St. Michael's Mount it shone: it shone on Beachy Head.
Far on the deep the Spaniard saw, along each southern shire,
Cape beyond cape, in endless range, those twinkling points of fire.
The fisher left his skiff to rock on Tamar's glittering waves:
The rugged miners poured to war from Mendip's sunless caves!
O'er Longleat's towers, o'er Cranbourne's oaks, the fiery herald
    flew:
He roused the shepherds of Stonehenge, the rangers of Beaulieu.

Right sharp and quick the bells all night rang out from Bristol
    town,
And ere the day three hundred horse had met on Clifton down;
The sentinel on Whitehall gate looked forth into the night,
And saw o'erhanging Richmond Hill the streak of blood-red light,
Then bugle's note and cannon's roar the deathlike silence broke,
And with one start, and with one cry, the royal city woke.
At once on all her stately gates arose the answering fires;
At once the wild alarum clashed from all her reeling spires;
From all the batteries of the Tower pealed loud the voice of fear;
And all the thousand masts of Thames sent back a louder cheer;

And from the furthest wards was heard the rush of hurrying
  feet,
And the broad streams of pikes and flags rushed down each roaring
  street;
And broader still became the blaze, and louder still the din,
As fast from every village round the horse came spurring in:

And eastward straight from wild Blackheath the warlike errand
 went,
And roused in many an ancient hall the gallant squires of Kent.
Southward from Surrey's pleasant hills flew those bright couriers
 forth ;
High on bleak Hampstead's swarthy moor they started for the
 north ;
And on, and on, without a pause, untired they bounded still :
All night from tower to tower they sprang ; they sprang from hill
 to hill :
Till the proud peak unfurled the flag o'er Darwin's rocky dales,
Till like volcanoes flared to heaven the stormy hills of Wales,
Till twelve fair counties saw the blaze on Malvern's lonely height,
Till streamed in crimson on the wind the Wrekin's crest of light,
Till broad and fierce the star came forth on Ely's stately fane,
And tower and hamlet rose in arms o'er all the boundless plain ;
Till Belvoir's lordly terraces the sign to Lincoln sent,
And Lincoln sped the message on o'er the wide vale of Trent ;
Till Skiddaw saw the fire that burned on Gaunt's embattled pile,
And the red glare on Skiddaw roused the burghers of Carlisle.

  . . . .

LORD MACAULAY.

MARY AMBREE

WHEN captaines couragious, whom death cold not daunte,
Did march to the siege of the citty of Gaunt,
They mustred their souldiers by two and by three,
And the formost in battle was Mary Ambree.

When the brave sergeant-major was slaine in her sight,
Who was her true lover, her joy, and delight,
Because he was slaine most treacherouslie
Then vowd to revenge him Mary Ambree.

She clothed herselfe from the top to the toe
In buffe of the bravest, most seemelye to showe ;
A faire shirt of mail then slipped on shee :
Was not this a brave bonny lasse, Mary Ambree ?

A helmett of proofe shee strait did provide,
A stronge arminge-sword shee girt by her side,
On her hand a goodly faire gauntlett put shee :
Was not this a brave bonny lasse, Mary Ambree ?

Then tooke shee her sworde and her targett in hand,
Bidding all such, as wold, to bee of her band ;
To wayte on her person came thousand and three :
Was not this a brave bonny lasse, Mary Ambree ?

' My soldiers,' she saith, ' soe valliant and bold,
Nowe followe your captaine, whom you doe beholde ;
Still formost in battell myselfe will I bee : '
Was not this a brave bonny lasse, Mary Ambree ?

Then cryed out her souldiers, and loude they did say,
' Soe well thou becomest this gallant array,
Thy harte and thy weapons so well do agree,
Noe mayden was ever like Mary Ambree.'

She cheared her souldiers, that foughten for life.
With ancyent and standard, with drum and with fife,
With brave clanging trumpetts, that sounded so free ;
Was not this a brave bonny lasse, Mary Ambree ?

' Before I will see the worst of you all
To come into danger of death or of thrall,
This hand and this life I will venture so free : '
Was not this a brave bonny lasse, Mary Ambree ?

Shee ledd upp her souldiers in battaile array,
Gainst three times theyr number by breake of the daye ;
Seven howers in skirmish continued shee :
Was not this a brave bonny lasse, Mary Ambree ?

She filled the skyes with the smoke of her shott,
And her enemyes bodyes with bulletts so hott ;
For one of her owne men a score killed shee :
Was not this a brave bonny lasse, Mary Ambree ?

And when her false gunner, to spoyle her intent,
Away all her pellets and powder had sent,
Straight with her keen weapon she slasht him in three :
Was not this a brave bonny lasse, Mary Ambree ?

Being falselye betrayed for lucre of hyre,
At length she was forced to make a retyre ;
Then her souldiers into a strong castle drew shee :
Was not this a brave bonny lasse, Mary Ambree ?

Her foes they besett her on everye side,
As thinking close siege shee cold never abide ;
To beate down the walles they all did decree :
But stoutlye deffyd them brave Mary Ambree.

Then tooke shee her sword and her targett in hand,
And mounting the walls all undaunted did stand,
There daring their captaines to match any three :
O what a brave captaine was Mary Ambree !

' Now saye, English captaine, what woldest thou give
To ransome thy selfe, which else must not live ?
Come yield thy selfe quicklye, or slaine thou must bee :
Then smiled sweetlye brave Mary Ambree.

' Ye captaines couragious, of valour so bold,
Whom thinke you before you now you doe behold ? '
' A knight, sir, of England, and captaine soe free,
Who shortlye with us a prisoner must bee.'

' No captaine of England ; behold in your sight
Two brests in my bosome, and therefore no knight :
Noe knight, sirs, of England, nor captaine you see,
But a poor simple mayden called Mary Ambree.'

' But art thou a woman, as thou dost declare,
Whose valor hath proved so undaunted in warre ?
If England doth yield such brave maydens as thee,
Full well may they conquer, faire Mary Ambree.'

The Prince of Great Parma heard of her renowne,
Who long had advanced for England's fair crowne ;
Hee wooed her and sued her his mistress to bee,
And offered rich presents to Mary Ambree.

But this virtuous mayden despised them all :
' 'Ile nere sell my honour for purple nor pall ;
A mayden of England, sir, never will bee
The wench of a monarcke,' quoth Mary Ambree.

Then to her owne country shee backe did returne,
Still holding the foes of faire England in scorne ;
Therfore English captaines of every degree
Sing forth the brave valours of Mary Ambree.

RELIQUES OF ANCIENT ENGLISH POETRY.

ELIZABETH OF BOHEMIA

YOU meaner beauties of the night,
  Which poorly satisfy our eyes
More by your number than your light,
  You common-people of the skies,
What are you when the Moon shall rise ?

Ye violets that first appear,
  By your pure purple mantles known,
Like the proud virgins of the year,
  As if the spring were all your own,—
What are you when the Rose is blown ?

Ye curious chanters of the wood,
  That warble forth dame Nature's lays,
Thinking your passions understood
  By your weak accents ; what's your praise
When Philomel her voice doth raise ?

So when my Mistress shall be seen
  In form and beauty of her mind,
By virtue first, then choice, a Queen,
  Tell me, if she were not design'd
Th' eclipse and glory of her kind ?

SIR H. WOTTON.

CHERRY RIPE

THERE is a garden in her face
   Where roses and white lilies blow;
A heavenly paradise is that place,
   Wherein all pleasant fruits do grow;
There cherries grow that none may buy,
Till Cherry Ripe themselves do cry.

Those cherries fairly do enclose
   Of orient pearl a double row,
Which when her lovely laughter shows,
   They look like rose-buds fill'd with snow:
Yet them no peer nor prince may buy,
Till Cherry Ripe themselves do cry.

Her eyes like angels watch them still;
   Her brows like bended bows do stand,
Threat'ning with piercing frowns to kill
   All that approach with eye or hand,
These sacred cherries to come nigh,
—Till Cherry Ripe themselves do cry!

ANON.

MORNING

PACK, clouds, away, and welcome day,
   With night we banish sorrow,
Sweet air blow soft, mount Lark aloft
   To give my Love good-morrow.
Wings from the wind, to please her mind,
   Notes from the Lark I'll borrow;
Bird prune thy wing, Nightingale sing,
   To give my Love good-morrow;
     To give my Love good-morrow
     Notes from them all I'll borrow.

Wake from thy nest, Robin Red-breast,
   Sing birds in every furrow,
And from each hill, let music shrill,
   Give my fair Love good-morrow :
Black-bird and thrush, in every bush,
   Stare, linnet, and cock-sparrow !
You pretty elves, amongst yourselves
   Sing my fair Love good-morrow.
      To give my Love good-morrow
      Sing birds in every furrow.

                  T. HEYWOOD.

DEATH THE LEVELLER

THE glories of our blood and state
   Are shadows, not substantial things ;
There is no armour against fate ;
   Death lays his icy hand on kings :
      Sceptre and Crown
      Must tumble down,
And in the dust be equal made
With the poor crooked scythe and spade.

Some men with swords may reap the field,
   And plant fresh laurels where they kill ;
But their strong nerves at last must yield ;
   They tame but one another still :
      Early or late
      They stoop to fate,
And must give up their murmuring breath,
When they, pale captives, creep to death.

The garlands wither on your brow,
   Then boast no more your mighty deeds ;
Upon Death's purple altar now,
   See where the victor-victim bleeds :
      Your heads must come
      To the cold tomb,
Only the actions of the just
Smell sweet, and blossom in their dust.

                  J. SHIRLEY.

ANNAN WATER

ANNAN Water's wading deep,
  And my Love Annie's wondrous bonny;
And I am loath she should wet her feet,
  Because I love her best of ony.'

He's loupen on his bonny gray,
  He rode the right gate and the ready;
For all the storm he wadna stay,
  For seeking of his bonny lady.

And he has ridden o'er field and fell,
  Through moor, and moss, and many a mire;
His spurs of steel were sair to bide,
  And from her four feet flew the fire.

' My bonny gray, now play your part !
  If ye be the steed that wins my dearie,
With corn and hay ye'll be fed for aye,
  And never spur shall make you wearie.'

The gray was a mare, and a right gude mare ,
  But when she wan the Annan Water,
She could not have ridden the ford that night
  Had a thousand merks been wadded at her.

'O boatman, boatman, put off your boat,
  Put off your boat for golden money ! '
But for all the gold in fair Scotland,
  He dared not take him through to Annie.

'O I was sworn so late yestreen,
  Not by a single oath, but mony !
I'll cross the drumly stream to-night,
  Or never could I face my honey.'

The side was stey, and the bottom deep,
  From bank to brae the water pouring;
The bonny gray mare she swat for fear,
  For she heard the water-kelpy roaring.

He spurr'd her forth into the flood,
  I wot she swam both strong and steady;
But the stream was broad, and her strength did fail,
  And he never saw his bonny lady!

UNKNOWN.

TO A WATERFOWL

WHITHER, 'midst falling dew,
While glow the heavens with the last steps of day,
Far through their rosy depths, dost thou pursue
    Thy solitary way?

Vainly the fowler's eye
Might mark thy distant flight to do thee wrong,
As, darkly painted on the crimson sky,
    Thy figure floats along.

Seek'st thou the plashy brink
Of weedy lake, or marge of river wide,
Or where the rocking billows rise and sink
    On the chafed ocean side?

There is a Power whose care
Teaches thy way along that pathless coast,—
The desert and illimitable air,—
    Lone wandering, but not lost.

All day thy wings have fann'd,
At that far height, the cold, thin atmosphere;
Yet stoop not, weary, to the welcome land,
    Though the dark night is near.

And soon that toil shall end;
Soon shalt thou find a summer home, and rest
And scream among thy fellows; reeds shall bend
Soon o'er thy shelter'd nest.

Thou'rt gone—the abyss of heaven
Hath swallow'd up thy form—yet on my heart
Deeply hath sunk the lesson thou hast given,
And shall not soon depart.

He, who from zone to zone
Guides through the boundless sky thy certain flight,
In the long way that I must tread alone,
Will lead my steps aright.

W. C. BRYANT.

SO, WE'LL GO NO MORE A ROVING

I

So, we'll go no more a roving
　　So late into the night,
Though the heart be still as loving,
　　And the moon be still as bright.

II

For the sword outwears its sheath,
　　And the soul wears out the breast,
And the heart must pause to breathe,
　　And love itself have rest.

III

Though the night was made for loving,
　　And the day returns too soon,
Yet we'll go no more a roving
　　By the light of the moon.

LORD BYRON.

SONG

WHERE the bee sucks, there suck I:
In a cowslip's bell I lie;
There I couch, when owls do cry:
On the bat's back I do fly
After summer merrily.
　　　　Merrily, merrily, shall I live now,
　　　　Under the blossom that hangs on the bough!

Come unto these yellow sands,
　　And then take hands:
Courtsied when you have and kiss'd
　　The wild waves whist,

Foot it featly here and there;
And, sweet Sprites, the burthen bear.
    Hark, hark!
        Bow-wow.
    The watch-dogs bark:
        Bow-wow.
    Hark, hark! I hear
The strain of strutting chanticleer
        Cry, Cock-a-diddle-dow!

W. SHAKESPEARE.

THE LAND O' THE LEAL

I'M wearin' awa', Jean,
Like snaw-wreaths in thaw, Jean,
I'm wearin' awa'
    To the land o' the leal.
There's nae sorrow there, Jean,
There's neither cauld nor care, Jean,
The day is aye fair
    In the land o' the leal.

Ye were aye leal and true, Jean,
Your task's ended noo, Jean,
And I'll welcome you
    To the land o' the leal.
Our bonnie bairn's there, Jean,
She was baith guid and fair, Jean;
O we grudged her right sair
    To the land o' the leal!

Then dry that tearfu' e'e, Jean,
My soul langs to be free, Jean,
And angels wait on me
    To the land o' the leal.
Now fare ye weel, my ain Jean,
This warld's care is vain, Jean;
We'll meet and aye be fain
    In the land o' the leal.

LADY NAIRNE.

SONG OF THE EMIGRANTS IN BERMUDA

WHERE the remote Bermudas ride
In the ocean's bosom unespied,
From a small boat that row'd along
The listening winds received this song:
' What should we do but sing His praise
That led us through the watery maze
Where He the huge sea-monsters wracks
That lift the deep upon their backs,
Unto an isle so long unknown,
And yet far kinder than our own?
He lands us on a grassy stage,
Safe from the storms, and prelate's rage:
He gave us this eternal spring
Which here enamels everything,
And sends the fowls to us in care
On daily visits through the air.
He hangs in shades the orange bright
Like golden lamps in a green night,
And does in the pomegranates close
Jewels more rich than Ormus shows:
He makes the figs our mouths to meet,
And throws the melons at our feet;
But apples plants of such a price,
No tree could ever bear them twice!
With cedars chosen by his hand
From Lebanon he stores the land;
And makes the hollow seas that roar
Proclaim the ambergris on shore.
He cast (of which we rather boast)
The Gospel's pearl upon our coast;
And in these rocks for us did frame
A temple where to sound His name.
O let our voice His praise exalt
Till it arrive at Heaven's vault,
Which then perhaps rebounding may
Echo beyond the Mexique bay!'

—Thus sung they in the English boat
A holy and a cheerful note :
And all the way, to guide their chime,
With falling oars they kept the time.

A. MARVELL.

THE LIGHT OF OTHER DAYS

OFT in the stilly night
  Ere slumber's chain has bound me,
Fond Memory brings the light
  Of other days around me :
    The smiles, the tears
    Of boyhood's years,
  The words of love then spoken ;
    The eyes that shone,
    Now dimmed and gone,
  The cheerful hearts now broken !
Thus in the stilly night
  Ere slumber's chain has bound me,
Sad Memory brings the light
  Of other days around me.

When I remember all
  The friends so link'd together
I've seen around me fall
  Like leaves in wintry weather,
    I feel like one
    Who treads alone
  Some banquet-hall deserted,
    Whose lights are fled,
    Whose garlands dead,
  And all but he departed !
Thus in the stilly night
  Ere slumber's chain has bound me,
Sad Memory brings the light
  Of other days around me.

T. MOORE.

THE FIRE OF DRIFT-WOOD

WE sat within the farm-house old,
  Whose windows, looking o'er the bay,
Gave to the sea-breeze, damp and cold,
  An easy entrance, night and day.

Not far away we saw the port,
  The strange, old-fashioned, silent town,
The light-house, the dismantled fort,
  The wooden houses, quaint and brown.

We sat and talked until the night,
  Descending, filled the little room;
Our faces faded from the sight,
  Our voices only broke the gloom.

We spake of many a vanished scene,
  Of what we once had thought and said,
Of what had been, and might have been,
  And who was changed, and who was dead;

And all that fills the hearts of friends,
  When first they feel, with secret pain,
Their lives thenceforth have separate ends,
  And never can be one again.

The first light swerving of the heart,
  That words are powerless to express,
And leave it still unsaid in part,
  Or say it in too great excess.

The very tones in which we spake
  Had something strange, I could but mark;
The leaves of memory seemed to make
  A mournful rustling in the dark.

Oft died the words upon our lips,
   As suddenly, from out the fire
Built of the wreck of stranded ships,
   The flames would leap and then expire.

And, as their splendour flashed and failed,
   We thought of wrecks upon the main,—
Of ships dismasted, that were hailed
   And sent no answer back again.

The windows, rattling in their frames,
   The ocean, roaring up the beach,
The gusty blast, the bickering flames,
   All mingled vaguely in our speech;

Until they made themselves a part
   Of fancies floating through the brain,
The long-lost ventures of the heart,
   That send no answers back again.

O flames that glowed! O hearts that yearned!
 They were indeed too much akin,
The drift wood fire without that burned,
 The thoughts that burned and glowed within.

H. W. LONGFELLOW.

THE WAR-SONG OF DINAS VAWR

THE mountain sheep are sweeter,
But the valley sheep are fatter;
We therefore deemed it meeter
To carry off the latter.
We made an expedition;
We met an host and quelled it;
We forced a strong position,
And killed the men who held it.

On Dyfed's richest valley,
Where herds of kine were browsing,
We made a mighty sally,
To furnish our carousing.
Fierce warriors rushed to meet us;
We met them, and o'erthrew them:
They struggled hard to beat us;
But we conquered them, and slew them.

As we drove our prize at leisure,
The king marched forth to catch us:
His rage surpassed all measure,
But his people could not match us.
He fled to his hall-pillars;
And, ere our force we led off,
Some sacked his house and cellars,
While others cut his head off.

We there, in strife bewildering,
Spilt blood enough to swim in,
We orphaned many children,
And widowed many women.

The eagles and the ravens
We glutted with our foemen
The heroes and the cravens,
The spearmen and the bowmen.

We brought away from battle,
And much their land bemoaned them,
Two thousand head of cattle,
And the head of him who owned them:
Ednyfed, King of Dyfed,
His head was borne before us;
His wine and beasts supplied our feasts,
And his overthrow, our chorus.

T. L. PEACOCK.

THE BEARD AND THE HAIR
OF THE RIVER-GOD WERE
SEEN THROUGH THE TORRENT'S SWEEP.

ARETHUSA

ARETHUSA arose
From her couch of snows
In the Acroceraunian moun-
　　tains,—
　From cloud and from crag,
　With many a jag
Shepherding her bright foun-
　　tains.
　She leapt down the rocks
　With her rainbow locks
Streaming among the streams;
　Her steps paved with green
　The downward ravine
Which slopes to the western
　　gleams:
　And gliding and springing,
　She went, ever singing,
In murmurs as soft as sleep.
　The Earth seemed to love her
　And Heaven smiled above her,
As she lingered towards the deep.

　Then Alpheus bold,
　On his glacier cold,
With his trident the mountains
　　strook,
　And opened a chasm
　In the rocks:—with the spasm
All Erymanthus shook.
　And the black south wind
　It concealed behind
The urns of the silent snow,
　And earthquake and thunder
　Did rend in sunder
　The bars of the springs below.
　The beard and the hair
　Of the River-god were

Seen　through　the　torrent's
　　sweep,
　As he followed the light
　Of the fleet Nymph's flight
To the brink of the Dorian deep.

'Oh, save me! Oh, guide me!
　And bid the deep hide me.
For he grasps me now by the
　　hair!'
　The loud Ocean heard,
　To its blue depth stirred,
And divided at her prayer;
　And under the water
　The Earth's white daughter
Fled like a sunny beam;
　Behind her descended,
　Her billows, unblended
With　the　brackish　Dorian
　　stream.
　Like a gloomy stain
　On the emerald main
Alpheus rushed behind,—
　As an eagle pursuing
　A dove to its ruin
Down the streams of the cloudy
　　wind.

Under the bowers
Where the Ocean Powers
Sit on their pearlèd thrones;
　Through the coral woods
　Of the weltering floods;
Over heaps of unvalued stones;
　Through the dim beams
　Which amid the streams

Weave a network of coloured
  light ;
  And under the caves,
  Where the shadowy waves
Are as green as the forest's
  night :
  Outspeeding the shark,
  And the swordfish dark,—
Under the ocean foam,
  And up through the rifts
  Of the mountain clifts,—
They passed to their Dorian
  home.

And now from their fountains
In Enna's mountains,

Down one vale where the morn-
  ing basks,
  Like friends once parted
  Grown single-hearted,
They ply their watery tasks.
  At sunrise they leap
  From their cradles steep
In the cave of the shelving hill;
  At noontide they flow
  Through the woods below
And the meadows of asphodel ;
  And at night they sleep
  In the rocking deep
Beneath the Ortygian shore,—
  Like spirits that lie
  In the azure sky
When they love but live no more.

P. B. SHELLEY.

THE DAY IS DONE

THE day is done, and the darkness
  Falls from the wings of Night,
As a feather is wafted downward
  From an eagle in his flight.

I see the lights of the village
  Gleam through the rain and the mist,
And a feeling of sadness comes o'er me,
  That my soul cannot resist ;

A feeling of sadness and longing,
  That is not akin to pain,
And resembles sorrow only
  As the mist resembles the rain.

Come, read to me some poem,
   Some simple and heartfelt lay,
That shall soothe this restless feeling,
   And banish the thoughts of day.

Not from the grand old masters,
   Not from the bards sublime,
Whose distant footsteps echo
   Through the corridors of Time.

For, like strains of martial music,
   Their mighty thoughts suggest
Life's endless toil and endeavour;
   And to-night I long for rest.

Read from some humbler poet,
   Whose songs gushed from his heart,
As showers from the clouds of summer,
   Or tears from the eyelids start;

Who, through long days of labour,
   And nights devoid of ease,
Still heard in his soul the music
   Of wonderful melodies.

Such songs have power to quiet
   The restless pulse of care,
And come like the benediction
   That follows after prayer.

Then read from the treasured volume
   The poem of thy choice,
And lend to the rhyme of the poet
   The beauty of thy voice.

And the night shall be filled with music,
   And the cares that infest the day
Shall fold their tents, like the Arabs,
   And as silently steal away.

                     H. W. LONGFELLOW.

SONG

A WEARY lot is thine, fair maid,
　A weary lot is thine !
To pull the thorn thy brow to braid,
　And press the rue for wine !

A lightsome eye, a soldier's mien,
　A feather of the blue,
A doublet of the Lincoln green,—
　No more of me you knew,
　　　　　My love !
No more of me you knew.

'This morn is merry June, I trow,
  The rose is budding fain;
But she shall bloom in winter snow,
  Ere we two meet again.'
He turn'd his charger as he spake,
  Upon the river shore,
He gave his bridle-reins a shake,
  Said, 'Adieu for evermore,
                    My love!
And adieu for evermore.'

SIR W. SCOTT.

THE TWO APRIL MORNINGS

WE walked along, while bright and red
  Uprose the morning sun:
And Matthew stopped, he looked, and said,
  'The will of God be done!'

A village schoolmaster was he,
  With hair of glittering grey;
As blithe a man as you could see
  On a spring holiday.

And on that morning, through the grass,
  And by the steaming rills,
We travelled merrily, to pass
  A day among the hills.

'Our work,' said I, 'was well begun;
  Then, from thy breast what thought,
Beneath so beautiful a sun,
  So sad a sigh has brought?'

A second time did Matthew stop;
  And fixing still his eye
Upon the eastern mountain-top,
  To me he made reply:

' Yon cloud with that long purple cleft
　　Brings fresh into my mind
A day like this which I have left
　　Full thirty years behind.

' And just above yon slope of corn
　　Such colours, and no other,
Were in the sky, that April morn,
　　Of this the very brother.

' With rod and line I sued the sport
    Which that sweet season gave,
And, to the church-yard come, stopped short
    Beside my daughter's grave.

' Nine summers had she scarcely seen,
    The pride of all the vale;
And then she sang;—she would have been
    A very nightingale.

' Six feet in earth my Emma lay;
    And yet I loved her more,
For so it seemed, than till that day
    I e'er had loved before.

' And, turning from her grave, I met,
    Beside the church-yard yew,
A blooming girl, whose hair was wet
    With points of morning dew.

' A basket on her head she bare;
    Her brow was smooth and white:
To see a child so very fair
    It was a pure delight!

' No fountain from its rocky cave
    E'er tripped with foot so free;
She seemed as happy as a wave
    That dances on the sea.

' There came from me a sigh of pain
    Which I could ill confine;
I looked at her, and looked again,
    And did not wish her mine! '

Matthew is in his grave, yet now,
    Methinks, I see him stand,
As at that moment, with a bough
    Of wilding in his hand.

                  W. WORDSWORTH.

TO HELEN

HELEN, thy beauty is to me
  Like those Nicèan barks of yore
That gently, o'er a perfumed sea,
  The weary wayworn wanderer bore
  To his own native shore.

On desperate seas long wont to roam,
  Thy hyacinth hair, thy classic face,
Thy Naiad airs have brought me home
  To the glory that was Greece,
To the grandeur that was Rome.

Lo, in yon brilliant window-niche,
  How statue-like I see thee stand,
  The agate lamp within thy hand!
Ah, Psyche, from the regions which
  Are holy land!

E. A. POE.

THE SKYLARK

BIRD of the wilderness,
  Blithesome and cumberless,
Sweet be thy matin o'er moorland and lea!
  Emblem of happiness,
  Blest is thy dwelling-place—
Oh, to abide in the desert with thee!

Wild is thy lay and loud,
  Far in the downy cloud,
Love gives it energy, love gave it birth.
  Where, on thy dewy wing,
  Where art thou journeying?
Thy lay is in heaven, thy love is on earth.

O'er fell and fountain sheen,
O'er moor and mountain green,
O'er the red streamer that heralds the day,
Over the cloudlet dim,
Over the rainbow's rim,
Musical cherub, soar, singing, away !

Then, when the gloaming comes,
Low in the heather blooms
Sweet will thy welcome and bed of love be !
Emblem of happiness,
Blest is thy dwelling-place —
Oh, to abide in the desert with thee !

J. HOGG.

FIDELE

FEAR no more the heat o' the sun
Nor the furious winter's rages ;
Thou thy worldly task hast done,
Home art gone and ta'en thy wages :
Golden lads and girls all must,
As chimney-sweepers, come to dust.

Fear no more the frown o' the great,
Thou art past the tyrant's stroke ;
Care no more to clothe, and eat ;
To thee the reed is as the oak :
The sceptre, learning, physic, must
All follow this, and come to dust.

Fear no more the lightning flash,
Nor the all-dreaded thunder-tone
Fear not slander, censure rash ;
Thou hast finish'd joy and moan
All lovers young, all lovers must
Consign to thee, and come to dust.

W. SHAKESPEARE.

CUMNOR HALL

THE dews of summer night did fall;
   The moon, sweet Regent of the sky,
Silver'd the walls of Cumnor Hall,
   And many an oak that grew thereby.

Now nought was heard beneath the skies,
   The sounds of busy life were still,
Save an unhappy lady's sighs
   That issued from that lonely pile.

' Leicester ! ' she cried, ' is this thy love
   That thou so oft hast sworn to me,
To leave me in this lonely grove,
   Immured in shameful privity ?

' No more thou com'st with lover's speed
   Thy once-belovèd bride to see ;
But, be she alive, or be she dead,
   I fear, stern Earl, 's the same to thee.

' Not so the usage I received
   When happy in my father's hall ;
No faithless husband then me grieved,
   No chilling fears did me appal.

' I rose up with the cheerful morn,
   No lark more blithe, no flower more gay ;
And like the bird that haunts the thorn
   So merrily sung the livelong day.

' If that my beauty is but small,
   Among court ladies all despised,
Why didst thou rend it from that hall,
   Where, scornful Earl ! it well was prized ?

' But, Leicester, or I much am wrong,
   Or 'tis not beauty lures thy vows ;
Rather, ambition's gilded crown
   Makes thee forget thy humble spouse.

' Then, Leicester, why,—again I plead,
   The injured surely may repine,—
Why didst thou wed a country maid,
   When some fair Princess might be thine ?

' Why didst thou praise my humble charms,
   And oh ! then leave them to decay ?
Why didst thou win me to thy arms,
   Then leave to mourn the livelong day ?

' The village maidens of the plain
   Salute me lowly as they go ;
Envious they mark my silken train,
   Nor think a Countess can have woe.

' How far less blest am I than them !
   Daily to pine and waste with care !
Like the poor plant, that, from its stem
   Divided, feels the chilling air.

' My spirits flag—my hopes decay—
   Still that dread death-bell smites my ear :
And many a boding seems to say,
   Countess, prepare, thy end is near ! '

Thus sore and sad that Lady grieved
   In Cumnor Hall so lone and drear ;
And many a heartfelt sigh she heaved,
   And let fall many a bitter tear.

And ere the dawn of day appear'd,
  In Cumnor Hall so lone and drear,
Full many a piercing scream was heard,
  And many a cry of mortal fear.

The death-bell thrice was heard to ring;
  An aerial voice was heard to call,
And thrice the raven flapp'd its wing
  Around the towers of Cumnor Hall.

The mastiff howl'd at village door,
  The oaks were shatter'd on the green;
Woe was the hour—for never more
  That hapless Countess e'er was seen!

And in that manor now no more
  Is cheerful feast and sprightly ball;
For ever since that dreary hour
  Have spirits haunted Cumnor Hall.

The village maids, with fearful glance,
  Avoid the ancient moss-grown wall;
Nor ever lead the merry dance
  Among the groves of Cumnor Hall.

Full many a traveller oft hath sigh'd,
  And pensive wept the Countess' fall,
As wand'ring onwards they've espied
  The haunted towers of Cumnor Hall.

W. F. MICKLE.

TO A SKYLARK

Hail to thee, blithe spirit !
Bird thou never wert—
That from heaven or near it
Pourest thy full heart
In profuse strains of unpremeditated art.

Higher still and higher
From the earth thou springest :
Like a cloud of fire,
The blue deep thou wingest,
And singing still dost soar, and soaring ever singest.

In the golden lightning
Of the sunken sun,
O'er which clouds are brightening,
Thou dost float and run,
Like an embodied joy whose race is just begun.

The pale purple even
Melts around thy flight ;
Like a star of heaven
In the broad daylight,
Thou art unseen, but yet I hear thy shrill delight —

Keen as are the arrows
Of that silver sphere
Whose intense lamp narrows
In the white dawn clear,
Until we hardly see, we feel, that it is there.

All the earth and air
With thy voice is loud,
As, when night is bare,
From one lonely cloud
The moon rains out her beams, and heaven is overflow'd.

What thou art we know not;
 What is most like thee?
From rainbow clouds there flow not
 Drops so bright to see
As from thy presence showers a rain of melody:—

Like a poet hidden
 In the light of thought,
Singing hymns unbidden,
 Till the world is wrought
To sympathy with hopes and fears it heeded not:

Like a high-born maiden
 In a palace tower,
Soothing her love-laden
 Soul in secret hour
With music sweet as love which overflows her bower:

Like a glow-worm golden
 In a dell of dew,
Scattering unbeholden
 Its aërial hue
Among the flowers and grass which screen it from
   the view:

Like a rose embowered
 In its own green leaves,
By warm winds deflower'd,
 Till the scent it gives
Makes faint with too much sweet these heavy-wingèd
   thieves.

Sound of vernal showers
 On the twinkling grass,
Rain-awaken'd flowers,
 All that ever was,
Joyous and clear and fresh,—thy music doth surpass.

Teach us, sprite or bird,
 What sweet thoughts are thine:
I have never heard
 Praise of love or wine
That panted forth a flood of rapture so divine.

Chorus hymeneal
  Or triumphal chaunt,
Match'd with thine, would be all
  But an empty vaunt—
A thing wherein we feel there is some hidden want.

What objects are the fountains
  Of thy happy strain ?
What fields, or waves, or mountains ?
  What shapes of sky or plain ?
What love of thine own kind ? what ignorance of pain ?

With thy clear keen joyance
  Languor cannot be :
Shadow of annoyance
  Never came near thee :
Thou lovest, but ne'er knew love's sad satiety.

Waking or asleep,
  Thou of death must deem
Things more true and deep
  Than we mortals dream,
Or how could thy notes flow in such a crystal stream ?

We look before and after,
  And pine for what is not :
Our sincerest laughter
  With some pain is fraught ;
Our sweetest songs are those that tell of saddest
      thought.

Yet, if we could scorn,
  Hate and pride, and fear ;
If we were things born
  Not to shed a tear,
I know not how thy joy we ever should come near.

Better than all measures
  Of delightful sound,
Better than all treasures
  That in books are found,
Thy skill to poet were, thou scorner of the ground !

Teach me half the gladness
  That thy brain must know ;
Such harmonious madness
  From my lips would flow
The world should listen then as I am listening now !

P. B. SHELLEY.

THE NIGHTINGALE

As it fell upon a day
In the merry month of May,
Sitting in a pleasant shade,
Which a grove of myrtles made,
Beasts did leap and birds did sing,
Trees did grow and plants did spring,
Everything did banish moan
Save the nightingale alone.
She, poor bird, as all forlorn,
Lean'd her breast against a thorn,
And there sung the dolefullest ditty
That to hear it was great pity.
Fie, fie, fie, now would she cry ;
Tereu, tereu, by-and-by :
That to hear her so complain
Scarce I could from tears refrain ;
For her griefs so lively shown
Made me think upon mine own.
—Ah, thought I, thou mourn'st in vain,
None takes pity on thy pain :
Senseless trees, they cannot hear thee,
Ruthless beasts, they will not cheer thee :
King Pandion, he is dead,
All thy friends are lapp'd in lead :
All thy fellow birds do sing
Careless of thy sorrowing :
Even so, poor bird, like·thee
None alive will pity me.

R. BARNEFIELD.

THE SLEEPER

At midnight, in the month of June,
I stand beneath the mystic moon:
An opiate vapour, dewy, dim,
Exhales from out her golden rim;
And, softly dripping, drop by drop,
Upon the quiet mountain top,
Steals drowsily and musically
Into the universal valley.
The rosemary nods upon the grave;
The lily lolls upon the wave;
Wrapping the fog about its breast,
The ruin moulders into rest;
Looking like Lethe, see, the lake
A conscious slumber seems to take,
And would not, for the world, awake.
All Beauty sleeps!—and, lo! where lies
(Her casement open to the skies)
Irene, with her destinies!

O, lady bright, can it be right,
This window open to the night?
The wanton airs from the tree-top,
Laughingly through the lattice drop;
The bodiless airs, a wizard rout,
Flit through thy chamber in and out,
And wave the curtain canopy
So fitfully, so fearfully,
Above the closed and fringèd lid
'Neath which thy slumb'ring soul lies hid,
That, o'er the floor and down the wall,
Like ghosts the shadows rise and fall!

Oh, lady dear, hast thou no fear?
Why and what art thou dreaming here?
Sure thou art come o'er far-off seas,
A wonder to these garden trees.
Strange is thy pallor, strange thy dress,
Strange, above all, thy length of tress,
And this all-solemn silentness.

The lady sleeps! Oh, may her sleep,
Which is enduring, so be deep!
Heaven have her in its sacred keep!
This chamber changed for one more holy,
This bed for one more melancholy,

I pray to God that she may lie
For ever with unopened eye,
While the dim sheeted ghosts go by !

My love, she sleeps !   O, may her sleep,
As it is lasting, so be deep !

Soft may the worms about her creep !
Far in the forest, dim and old,
For her may some tall vault unfold—
Some vault that oft hath flung its black
And wingèd panels fluttering back

P

Triumphant o'er the crested palls
Of her grand family funerals ;
Some sepulchre remote, alone,
Against whose portal she had thrown,
In childhood many an idle stone ;
Some tomb from out whose sounding door
She ne'er shall force an echo more,
Thrilling to think, poor child of sin,
It was the dead who groaned within.

E. A. POE.

SPRING

SPRING, the sweet Spring, is the year's pleasant king;
Then blooms each thing, then maids dance in a ring,
Cold doth not sting, the pretty birds do sing,
   Cuckoo, jug-jug, pu-we, to-witta-woo!

The palm and may make country houses gay,
Lambs frisk and play, the shepherds pipe all day,
And we hear aye, birds tune this merry lay,
   Cuckoo, jug-jug, pu-we, to-witta-woo!

The fields breathe sweet, the daisies kiss our feet,
Young lovers meet, old wives a-sunning sit,
In every street, these tunes our ears do greet,
   Cuckoo, jug-jug, pu-we, to-witta-woo!
      Spring! the sweet Spring!

T. NASHE.

THE BATTLE OF NASEBY

(BY OBADIAH BIND-THEIR-KINGS-IN-CHAINS-AND-THEIR-NOBLES-WITH
LINKS-OF-IRON, SERGEANT IN IRETON'S REGIMENT)

OH! wherefore come ye forth, in triumph from the North,
    With your hands, and your feet, and your raiment all red?
And wherefore doth your rout send forth a joyous shout?
    And whence be the grapes of the wine-press which ye tread?

Oh evil was the root, and bitter was the fruit,
    And crimson was the juice of the vintage that we trod;
For we trampled on the throng of the haughty and the strong,
    Who sate in the high places, and slew the saints of God.

It was about the noon of a glorious day of June,
    That we saw their banners dance, and their cuirasses shine,
And the Man of Blood was there, with his long essenced hair,
    And Astley, and Sir Marmaduke, and Rupert of the Rhine.

Like a servant of the Lord, with his Bible and his sword,
    The General rode along us to form us to the fight,
When a murmuring sound broke out, and swell'd into a shout
    Among the godless horsemen upon the tyrant's right.

And hark ! like the roar of the billows on the shore,
  The cry of battle rises along their charging line !
For God ! for the Cause ! for the Church, for the Laws !
  For Charles King of England, and Rupert of the Rhine !

The furious German comes, with his clarions and his drums,
  His bravoes of Alsatia, and pages of Whitehall ;
They are bursting on our flanks. Grasp your pikes, close your ranks,
  For Rupert never comes but to conquer or to fall.

They are here ! They rush on ! We are broken ! We are gone !
  Our left is borne before them like stubble on the blast.
O Lord, put forth thy might ! O Lord, defend the right !
  Stand back to back, in God's name, and fight it to the last.

Stout Skippon hath a wound ; the centre hath given ground :
  Hark ! hark !—What means the trampling of horsemen on our
    rear ?
Whose banner do I see, boys ? 'Tis he, thank God, 'tis he, boys.
  Bear up another minute : brave Oliver is here.

Their heads all stooping low, their points all in a row,
  Like a whirlwind on the trees, like a deluge on the dykes,
Our cuirassiers have burst on the ranks of the Accurst,
  And at a shock have scattered the forest of his pikes.

Fast, fast, the gallants ride, in some safe nook to hide
  Their coward heads, predestined to rot on Temple Bar :
And he—he turns, he flies :—shame on those cruel eyes
  That bore to look on torture, and dare not look on war.

Ho ! comrades, scour the plain ; and, ere ye strip the slain,
  First give another stab to make your search secure,
Then shake from sleeves and pockets their broad-pieces and lockets,
  The tokens of the wanton, the plunder of the poor.

Fools ! your doublets shone with gold, and your hearts were gay
    and bold,
  When you kissed your lily hands to your lemans to-day ;
And to-morrow shall the fox, from her chambers in the rocks,
  Lead forth her tawny cubs to howl above the prey.

Where be your tongues that late mocked at heaven and hell and fate,
   And the fingers that once were so busy with your blades,
Your perfum'd satin clothes, your catches and your oaths,
   Your stage-plays and your sonnets, your diamonds and your
      spades ?

Down, down, for ever down with the mitre and the crown,
   With the Belial of the Court, and the Mammon of the Pope ;
There is woe in Oxford Halls ; there is wail in Durham's Stalls :
   The Jesuit smites his bosom : the Bishop rends his cope.

And She of the seven hills shall mourn her children's ills,
   And tremble when she thinks on the edge of England's sword ;
And the Kings of earth in fear shall shudder when they hear
   What the hand of God hath wrought for the Houses and the Word.

LORD MACAULAY.

ROSABELLE

O LISTEN, listen, ladies gay !
   No haughty feat of arms I tell ;
Soft is the note, and sad the lay,
   That mourns the lovely Rosabelle.

' Moor, moor the barge, ye gallant crew !
   And, gentle ladye, deign to stay !
Rest thee in Castle Ravensheuch,
   Nor tempt the stormy firth to-day.

' The blackening wave is edged with white ;
   To inch [1] and rock the sea-mews fly ;
The fishers have heard the Water-Sprite,
   Whose screams forebode that wreck is nigh.

' Last night the gifted Seer did view
   A wet shroud swathed round ladye gay ;
Then stay thee, Fair, in Ravensheuch ;
   Why cross the gloomy firth to-day ? '—

[1] *Inch*, isle.

' 'Tis not because Lord Lindesay's heir
　　To-night at Roslin leads the ball,
But that my ladye-mother there
　　Sits lonely in her castle-hall.

' 'Tis not because the ring they ride,
　　And Lindesay at the ring rides well,
But that my sire the wine will chide,
　　If 'tis not fill'd by Rosabelle.'—

O'er Roslin all that dreary night,
　　A wondrous blaze was seen to gleam;
'Twas broader than the watch-fire's light,
　　And redder than the bright moonbeam.

It glared on Roslin's castled rock,
　　It ruddied all the copse-wood glen;
'Twas seen from Dryden's groves of oak,
　　And seen from cavern'd Hawthornden.

Seem'd all on fire that chapel proud,
　　Where Roslin's chiefs uncoffin'd lie,
Each Baron, for a sable shroud,
　　Sheathed in his iron panoply.

Seem'd all on fire within, around,
　　Deep sacristy and altar's pale;
Shone every pillar foliage-bound,
　　And glimmer'd all the dead men's mail.

Blazed battlement and pinnet high,
　　Blazed every rose-carved buttress fair—
So still they blaze, when fate is nigh
　　The lordly line of high St. Clair.

There are twenty of Roslin's barons bold
　　Lie buried within that proud chapelle;
Each one the holy vault doth hold—
　　But the sea holds lovely Rosabelle!

And each St. Clair was buried there,
  With candle, with book, and with knell ;
But the sea-caves rung, and the wild wings sung,
  The dirge of lovely Rosabelle !

SIR W. SCOTT.

THE RIME OF THE ANCIENT MARINER

IN SEVEN PARTS

PART I

IT is an ancient Mariner,
And he stoppeth one of three.
' By thy long grey beard and glittering eye,
Now wherefore stopp'st thou me ?

 The Bridegroom's doors are open'd wide,
And I am next of kin ;
The guests are met, the feast is set :
May'st hear the merry din.'

He holds him with his skinny hand,
' There was a ship,' quoth he.
' Hold off ! unhand me, grey-beard loon ! '
Eftsoons his hand dropt he.

He holds him with his glittering eye—
The Wedding-Guest stood still,
And listens like a three years' child :
The Mariner hath his will.

The Wedding-Guest sat on a stone :
He cannot choose but hear ;
And thus spake on that ancient man,
The bright-eyed Mariner :

' The ship was cheer'd, the harbour clear'd,
Merrily did we drop
Below the kirk, below the hill,
Below the light-house top.

' The Sun came up upon the left,
Out of the sea came he !
And he shone bright, and on the right
Went down into the sea.

' Higher and higher every day
Till over the mast at noon—'
The Wedding-Guest here beat his breast
For he heard the loud bassoon.

The Bride hath paced into the hall,
Red as a rose is she ;
Nodding their heads before her goes
The merry minstrelsy.

The Wedding-Guest he beat his breast,
Yet he cannot choose but hear ;
And thus spake on that ancient man,
The bright-eyed Mariner :

' And now the storm-blast came, and he
Was tyrannous and strong :
He struck with his o'ertaking wings,
And chased us south along.

' With sloping masts and dipping prow,
As who pursued with yell and blow
Still treads the shadow of his foe,
And forward bends his head,
The ship drove fast, loud roar'd the blast,
And southward aye we fled.

' And now there came both mist and snow,
And it grew wondrous cold :
And ice, mast high, came floating by,
As green as emerald.

'And through the drifts the snowy clifts
Did send a dismal sheen :
Nor shapes of men nor beasts we ken—
The ice was all between.

'The ice was here, the ice was there,
The ice was all around :
It crack'd and growl'd, and roar'd and howl'd,
Like noises in a swound !

'At length did cross an Albatross,
Thorough the fog it came ;
As if it had been a Christian soul
We hail'd it in God's name.

'It ate the food it ne'er had eat,
And round and round it flew.
The ice did split with a thunder-fit ;
The helmsman steer'd us through.

'And a good south wind sprung up behind ;
The Albatross did follow,
And every day, for food or play,
Came to the mariners' hollo !

'In mist or cloud, on mast or shroud,
It perch'd for vespers nine ;
Whiles all the night, through fog-smoke white,
Glimmer'd the white moon-shine.'

'God save thee, ancient Mariner !
From the fiends, that plague thee thus !—
Why look'st thou so ? '—' With my cross-bow
I shot the Albatross ! '

PART II

'The Sun now rose upon the right :
Out of the sea came he,
Still hid in mist, and on the left
Went down into the sea.

' And the good south wind still blew behind,
But no sweet bird did follow,
Nor any day for food or play
Came to the mariners' hollo !

' And I had done a hellish thing,
And it would work 'em woe :
For all averr'd, I had kill'd the bird
That made the breeze to blow.
Ah wretch ! said they, the bird to slay,
That made the breeze to blow !

' Nor dim nor red, like God's own head,
The glorious Sun uprist :
Then all averr'd, I had kill'd the bird
That brought the fog and mist.
'Twas right, said they, such birds to slay,
That bring the fog and mist.

' The fair breeze blew, the white foam flew,
The furrow stream'd off free ;
We were the first that ever burst
Into that silent sea.

' Down dropt the breeze, the sails dropt down
'Twas sad as sad could be ;
And we did speak only to break
The silence of the sea !

' All in a hot and copper sky,
The bloody Sun, at noon,
Right up above the mast did stand,
No bigger than the Moon.

' Day after day, day after day,
We struck, nor breath nor motion ;
As idle as a painted ship
Upon a painted ocean.

' Water, water, everywhere,
And all the boards did shrink ;
Water, water, everywhere,
Nor any drop to drink.

' The very deep did rot : O Christ !
That ever this should be !
Yea, slimy things did crawl with legs
Upon the slimy sea.

' About, about, in reel and rout
The death-fires danced at night ;
The water, like a witch's oils,
Burnt green and blue, and white.

' And some in dreams assured were
Of the spirit that plagued us so ;
Nine fathom deep he had followed us
From the land of mist and snow.

' And every tongue, through utter drought,
Was wither'd at the root ;
We could not speak, no more than if
We had been choked with soot.

' Ah ! well a-day ! what evil looks
Had I from old and young !
Instead of the Cross, the Albatross
About my neck was hung. '

PART III

' There pass'd a weary time.   Each throat
Was parch'd, and glazed each eye.
A weary time !   A weary time !
How glazed each weary eye !
When looking westward, I beheld
A something in the sky.

' At first it seem'd a little speck,
And then it seem'd a mist ;
It moved and moved, and took at last
A certain shape, I wist.

' A speck, a mist, a shape, I wist !
And still it near'd and near'd :
As if it dodged a water-sprite,
It plunged and tack'd and veered.

THE DEATH-FIRES DANCED AT NIGHT.

‘ With throats unslaked, with black lips baked,
We could nor laugh nor wail ;
Through utter drought all dumb we stood !
I bit my arm, I suck’d the blood,
And cried, “A sail ! a sail ! ”

‘ With throats unslaked, with black lips baked,
Agape they heard me call :
Gramercy ! they for joy did grin,
And all at once their breath drew in,
As they were drinking all.

‘ See ! see ! (I cried) she tacks no more !
Hither to work us weal ;
Without a breeze, without a tide,
She steadies with upright keel !

‘ The western wave was all a-flame,
The day was well-nigh done !

Almost upon the western wave
Rested the broad bright Sun;
When that strange shape drove suddenly
Betwixt us and the Sun.

'And straight the Sun was fleck'd with bars,
(Heaven's Mother send us grace!)
As if through a dungeon-grate he peered,
With broad and burning face.

'Alas! (thought I, and my heart beat loud)
How fast she nears and nears!
Are those *her* sails that glance in the Sun,
Like restless gossameres?

" Are those *her* ribs through which the Sun
Did peer, as through a grate?
And is that Woman all her crew?
Is that a Death? and are there two?
Is Death that woman's mate?

· Her lips were red, her looks were free,
Her locks were yellow as gold:
Her skin was as white as leprosy,
The Night-mare Life-in-Death was she,
Who thicks man's blood with cold.

'The naked hulk alongside came,
And the twain were casting dice;
"The game is done! I've won, I've won!"
Quoth she, and whistles thrice.

'The Sun's rim dips; the stars rush out;
At one stride comes the dark;
With far-heard whisper, o'er the sea
Off shot the spectre-bark.

' We listen'd and look'd sideways up!
Fear at my heart, as at a cup,

My life-blood seem'd to sip!
The stars were dim, and thick the night,
The steersman's face by his lamp gleam'd white;

From the sails the dew did drip—
Till clomb above the eastern bar
The horned Moon, with one bright star
Within the nether tip.

' One after one, by the star-dogg'd Moon,
Too quick for groan or sigh,
Each turn'd his face with a ghastly pang,
And cursed me with his eye.

' Four times fifty living men,
(And I heard nor sigh nor groan)
With heavy thump, a lifeless lump,
They dropped down one by one.

' The souls did from their bodies fly,—
They fled to bliss or woe !
And every soul, it pass'd me by,
Like the whizz of my cross-bow ! '

PART IV

' I fear thee, ancient Mariner !
I fear thy skinny hand !
And thou art long, and lank, and brown,
As is the ribbed sea-sand.

' I fear thee and thy glittering eye,
And thy skinny hand, so brown.'—
' Fear not, fear not, thou Wedding-Guest !
This body dropt not down.

' Alone, alone, all all alone,
Alone on a wide, wide sea !
And never a saint took pity on
My soul in agony.

' The many men, so beautiful !
And they all dead did lie :
And a thousand thousand slimy things
Lived on ; and so did I.

' I look'd upon the rotting sea,
And drew my eyes away ;
I look'd upon the rotting deck,
And there the dead men lay.

'I look'd to Heaven, and tried to pray ;
But or ever a prayer had gusht,
A wicked whisper came, and made
My heart as dry as dust.

'I closed my lids, and kept them close,
And the balls like pulses beat ;
For the sky and the sea, and the sea and the sky
Lay like a load on my weary eye,
And the dead were at my feet.

Q

'The cold sweat melted from their limbs,
Nor rot nor reek did they:
The look with which they look'd on me
Had never pass'd away.

'An orphan's curse would drag to Hell
A spirit from on high;
But oh! more horrible than that
Is the curse in a dead man's eye!
Seven days, seven nights, I saw that curse,
And yet I could not die.

'The moving Moon went up the sky,
And nowhere did abide:
Softly she was going up,
And a star or two beside—
Her beams bemock'd the sultry main,
Like April hoar-frost spread;
But where the ship's huge shadow lay,
The charmèd water burnt alway
A still and awful red,

' Beyond the shadow of the ship,
I watched the water-snakes:
They moved in tracks of shining white,
And when they rear'd, the elfish light
Fell off in hoary flakes.

' Within the shadow of the ship
I watched their rich attire:
Blue, glossy green, and velvet black,
They coil'd and swam; and every track
Was a flash of golden fire.

' O happy living things! no tongue
Their beauty might declare:
A spring of love gush'd from my heart,
And I bless'd them unaware!
Sure my kind saint took pity on me,
And I bless'd them unaware!

' The self-same moment I could pray;
And from my neck so free
The Albatross fell off, and sank
Like lead into the sea.'

PART V

' Oh sleep! it is a gentle thing,
Beloved from pole to pole!
To Mary Queen the praise be given!
She sent the gentle sleep from Heaven,
That slid into my soul.

' The silly buckets on the deck,
That had so long remain'd,
I dreamt that they were fill'd with dew;
And when I awoke, it rained.

' My lips were wet, my throat was cold,
My garments all were dank;
Sure I had drunken in my dreams,
And still my body drank.

'I moved, and could not feel my limbs :
I was so light—almost
I thought that I had died in sleep,
And was a blessed ghost.

' And soon I heard a roaring wind :
It did not come anear ;
But with its sound it shook the sails,
That were so thin and sere.

' The upper air burst into life !
And a hundred fire-flags sheen,
To and fro they were hurried about !
And to and fro, and in and out,
The wan stars danced between.

' And the coming wind did roar more loud,
And the sails did sigh like sedge ;
And the rain pour'd down from one black cloud,
The Moon was at its edge.

' The thick black cloud was cleft and still,
The Moon was at its side :
Like waters shot from some high crag,
The lightning fell with never a jag,
A river steep and wide.

' The loud wind never reached the ship,
Yet now the ship moved on !
Beneath the lightning and the moon
The dead men gave a groan.

' They groan'd, they stirred, they all uprose,
Nor spake, nor moved their eyes ;
It had been strange, even in a dream,
To have seen those dead men rise.

' The helmsman steered, the ship moved on :
Yet never a breeze up blew ;
The mariners all 'gan work the ropes,
Where they were wont to do ;
They raised their limbs like lifeless tools—
We were a ghastly crew.

'The body of my brother's son
Stood by me, knee to knee :
The body and I pull'd at one rope,
But he said nought to me.'

'I fear thee, ancient Mariner!'
'Be calm, thou Wedding-Guest!
'Twas not those souls that fled in pain,
Which to their corses came again,
But a troop of spirits blest:
For when it dawn'd—they dropp'd their arms,
And cluster'd round the mast;
Sweet sounds rose slowly through their mouths,
And from their bodies passed.

'Around, around, flew each sweet sound,
Then darted to the Sun;
Slowly the sounds came back again,
Now mixed, now one by one.

'Sometimes a-dropping from the sky
I heard the sky-lark sing;
Sometimes all little birds that are,
How they seem'd to fill the sea and air
With their sweet jargoning!

'And now 'twas like all instruments,
Now like a lonely flute;
And now it is an angel's song,
That makes the heavens be mute.

'It ceased; yet still the sails made on
A pleasant noise till noon,
A noise like of a hidden brook
In the leafy month of June,
That to the sleeping woods all night
Singeth a quiet tune.

'Till noon we quietly sailed on,
Yet never a breeze did breathe:
Slowly and smoothly went the ship,
Moved onward from beneath.

Under the keel nine fathom deep,
From the land of mist and snow,
The spirit slid : and it was he
That made the ship to go.
The sails at noon left off their tune
And the ship stood still also.

'The Sun, right up above the mast,
Had fixed her to the ocean;
But in a minute she 'gan stir,
With a short uneasy motion—
Backwards and forwards half her length
With a short uneasy motion.

'Then like a pawing horse let go,
She made a sudden bound :
It flung the blood into my head,
And I fell down in a swound.

' How long in that same fit I lay,
I have not to declare ;
But ere my living life returned,
I heard, and in my soul discerned
Two voices in the air.

'" Is it he ? " quoth one, " Is this the man ?
By Him who died on cross,
With his cruel bow he laid full low
The harmless Albatross.

' " The spirit who bideth by himself
In the land of mist and snow,
He loved the bird that loved the man
Who shot him with his bow."

' The other was a softer voice,
As soft as honey-dew ;
Quoth he, " The man hath penance done,
And penance more will do.' "

PART VI

First Voice

' " But tell me, tell me ! speak again,
Thy soft response renewing—
What makes that ship drive on so fast ?
What is the Ocean doing ? "

Second Voice

' " Still as a slave before his lord,
The Ocean hath no blast ;
His great bright eye most silently
Up to the Moon is cast--

' " If he may know which way to go ;
For she guides him smooth or grim.
See, brother, see ! how graciously
She looketh down on him."

First Voice

' " But why drives on that ship so fast,
Without or wave or wind ? "

Second Voice

' " The air is cut away before,
And closes from behind.

· " Fly, brother, fly ! more high, more high !
Or we shall be belated
For slow and slow that ship will go,
When the Mariner's trance is abated."

' I woke, and we were sailing on
As in a gentle weather :
'Twas night, calm night, the Moon was high ;
The dead men stood together.

' All stood together on the deck,
For a charnel-dungeon fitter :
All fixed on me their stony eyes,
That in the Moon did glitter.

' The pang, the curse, with which they died,
Had never passed away :
I could not draw my eyes from theirs,
Nor turn them up to pray.

' And now this spell was snapt: once more
I view'd the ocean green,
And look'd far forth, yet little saw
Of what had else been seen—

' Like one that on a lonesome road
Doth walk in fear and dread,
And having once turned round walks on,
And turns no more his head ;
Because he knows, a frighful fiend
Doth close behind him tread.

' But soon there breathed a wind on me
Nor sound nor motion made :
Its path was not upon the sea,
In ripple or in shade.

' It raised my hair, it fann'd my cheek
Like a meadow-gale of spring—
It mingled strangely with my fears,
Yet it felt like a welcoming.

' Swiftly, swiftly flew the ship,
Yet she sail'd softly too :
Sweetly, sweetly blew the breeze—
On me alone it blew.

' Oh ! dream of joy ! is this indeed
The light-house top I see ?
Is this the hill ? is this the kirk ?
Is this mine own countree ?

'We drifted o'er the harbour-bar,
And I with sobs did pray—
"O let me be awake, my God!
Or let me sleep alway."

'The harbour bay was clear as glass,
So smoothly it was strewn!
And on the bay the moonlight lay,
And the shadow of the moon.

'The rock shone bright, the kirk no less,
That stands above the rock:
The moonlight steeped in silentness,
The steady weathercock.

'And the bay was white with silent light
Till, rising from the same,
Full many shapes, that shadows were,
In crimson colours came.

'A little distance from the prow
Those crimson shadows were:
I turned my eyes upon the deck—
Oh, Christ! what saw I there!

'Each corse lay flat, lifeless and flat,
And by the holy rood!
A man all light, a seraph-man,
On every corse there stood.

'This seraph-band, each waved his hand,
It was a heavenly sight!
They stood as signals to the land,
Each one a lovely light;

'This seraph-band, each waved his hand,
No voice did they impart—
No voice; but oh! the silence sank
Like music on my heart.

' But soon I heard the dash of oars,
I heard the Pilot's cheer ;
My head was turn'd perforce away,
And I saw a boat appear.

' The Pilot, and the Pilot's boy,
I heard them coming fast :
Dear Lord in Heaven ! it was a joy
The dead men could not blast.

' I saw a third—I heard his voice :
It is the Hermit good !
He singeth loud his godly hymns
That he makes in the wood.
He'll shrieve my soul, he'll wash away
The Albatross's blood.'

PART VII

' This Hermit good lives in that wood
Which slopes down to the sea.
How loudly his sweet voice he rears !
He loves to talk with marineres
That come from a far countree.

' He kneels at morn, and noon, and eve—
He hath a cushion plump :
It is the moss that wholly hides
The rotted old oak stump.

' The skiff-boat near'd : I heard them talk,
" Why, this is strange, I trow !
Where are those lights so many and fair,
That signal made but now ? "

' " Strange, by my faith ! " the Hermit said—
" And they answer'd not our cheer !
The planks look warp'd ! and see those sails,
How thin they are and sere !
I never saw aught like to them,
Unless perchance it were

‘ “ Brown skeletons of leaves that lag
My forest-brook along ;
When the ivy-tod is heavy with snow,
And the owlet whoops to the wolf below,
That eats the she-wolf's young.”

‘ “ Dear Lord ! it hath a fiendish look ”—
(The Pilot made reply)
“ I am a-fear'd ”—“ Push on, push on ! ”
Said the Hermit cheerily.

‘ The boat came closer to the ship,
But I nor spake nor stirred ;
The boat came close beneath the ship,
And straight a sound was heard.

‘ Under the water it rumbled on,
Still louder and more dread :
It reach'd the ship, it split the bay :
The ship went down like lead.

‘ Stunn'd by that loud and dreadful sound,
Which sky and ocean smote,
Like one that hath been seven days drowned
My body lay afloat ;
But swift as dreams, myself I found
Within the Pilot's boat.

‘ Upon the whirl, where sank the ship,
The boat spun round and round ;
And all was still, save that the hill
Was telling of the sound.

‘ I moved my lips—the Pilot shriek'd
And fell down in a fit ;
The holy Hermit raised his eyes,
And prayed where he did sit.

‘ I took the oars: the Pilot's boy,
Who now doth crazy go,
Laugh'd loud and long, and all the while
His eyes went to and fro.
“ Ha ! ha !” quoth he, “ full plain I see
The Devil knows how to row.’

' And now, all in my own countree,
I stood on the firm land !
The Hermit stepped forth from the boat,
And scarcely he could stand.

' "O shrieve me, shrieve me, holy man ! "
The Hermit crossed his brow.
" Say quick," quoth he, " I bid thee say—
What manner of man art thou ? "

' Forthwith this frame of mine was wrenched
With a woful agony,
Which forced me to begin my tale ;
And then· it left me free.

' Since then, at an uncertain hour,
That agony returns ;
And till my ghastly tale is told,
This heart within me burns.

' I pass, like night, from land to land ;
I have strange power of speech ;
The moment that his face I see,
I know the man that must hear me :
To him my tale I teach.

' What loud uproar bursts from that door !
The wedding-guests are there :
But in the garden-bower the bride
And bride-maids singing are :
And hark the little vesper bell,
Which biddeth me to prayer !

' O Wedding-Guest ! this soul hath been
Alone on a wide, wide sea :
So lonely 'twas, that God himself
Scarce seemèd there to be.

' O sweeter than the marriage-feast,
'Tis sweeter far to me,
To walk together to the kirk
With a goodly company !—

'To walk together to the kirk,
And all together pray,
While each to his great Father bends,
Old men, and babes, and loving friends,
And youths and maidens gay!

'Farewell, farewell! but this I tell
To thee, thou Wedding-Guest!
He prayeth well, who loveth well
Both man and bird and beast.

'He prayeth best, who loveth best
All things both great and small;
For the dear God who loveth us,
He made and loveth all.'

The Mariner, whose eye is bright,
Whose beard with age is hoar,
Is gone: and now the Wedding-Guest
Turned from the bridegroom's door.

He went like one that hath been stunned,
And is of sense forlorn:
A sadder and a wiser man
He rose the morrow morn.

S. T. COLERIDGE.

THE HAUNTED PALACE

I

IN the greenest of our valleys,
    By good angels tenanted,
Once a fair and stately palace,
    Radiant palace, reared its head.
In the monarch Thought's dominion,
    It stood there;
Never seraph spread a pinion
    Over fabric half so fair!

II

Banners—yellow, glorious, golden—
  On its roof did float and flow
(This, all this, was in the olden
  Time, long ago);
And every gentle air that dallied,
  In that sweet day,
Along the ramparts plumed and pallid,
  A wingèd odour went away.

III

Wanderers in that happy valley,
  Through two luminous windows saw
Spirits moving musically,
  To a lute's well-tunèd law,
Round about a throne where, sitting
  (Porphyrogene !)
In state his glory well befitting,
  The ruler of the realm was seen.

IV

And all with pearl and ruby glowing
  Was the fair palace-door,
Through which came flowing, flowing, flowing,
  And sparkling evermore,
A troop of Echoes, whose sweet duty
  Was but to sing,
In voices of surpassing beauty,
  The wit and wisdom of their king.

V

But evil things, in robes of sorrow,
  Assailed the monarch's high estate.
(Ah, let us mourn !—for never morrow
  Shall dawn upon him desolate ;)
And round about his home the glory
  That blushed and bloomed,
Is but a dim-remembered story
  Of the old time entombed.

VI

And travellers now within that valley,
   Through the red-litten windows see
Vast forms, that move fantastically
   To a discordant melody,

While, like a ghastly rapid river,
  Through the pale door
A hideous throng rush out for ever
  And laugh—but smile no more.

E. A. Poe.

THE BARD

PINDARIC ODE

' Ruin seize thee, ruthless King!
  Confusion on thy banners wait,
Tho' fann'd by Conquest's crimson wing
  They mock the air with idle state.
Helm, nor Hauberk's twisted mail,
Nor e'en thy virtues, Tyrant, shall avail
To save thy secret soul from nightly fears,
From Cambria's curse, from Cambria's tears!'
—Such were the sounds, that o'er the crested pride
  Of the first Edward scatter'd wild dismay,
As down the steep of Snowdon's shaggy side
  He wound with toilsome march his long array.
Stout Glo'ster stood aghast in speechless trance:
'To arms!' cried Mortimer, and couch'd his quivering lance.

On a rock, whose haughty brow
Frowns o'er old Conway's foaming flood,
  Robed in the sable garb of woe,
With haggard eyes the Poet stood;
(Loose his beard and hoary hair
Stream'd like a meteor to the troubled air)
  And with a Master's hand and Prophet's fire
Struck the deep sorrows of his lyre.
' Hark, how each giant-oak and desert cave
  Sigh's to the torrent's aweful voice beneath!
O'er thee, oh King! their hundred arms they wave,
  Revenge on thee in hoarser murmurs breathe;
Vocal no more, since Cambria's fatal day,
To high-born Hoel's harp, or soft Llewellyn's lay,

R 2

' Cold is Cadwallo's tongue,
 That hush'd the stormy main :
Brave Urien sleeps upon his craggy bed :
 Mountains, ye mourn in vain
 Modred, whose magic song
Made huge Plinlimmon bow his cloud-topp'd head.
 On dreary Arvon's shore they lie,
Smear'd with gore, and ghastly pale :
Far, far aloof th' affrighted ravens sail ;
 The famish'd Eagle screams, and passes by.
Dear lost companions of my tuneful art,
 Dear, as the light that visits these sad eyes,
Dear, as the ruddy drops that warm my heart,
 Ye died amidst your dying country's cries—
No more I weep. They do not sleep.
 On yonder cliffs, a griesly band,
I see them sit, they linger yet,
 Avengers of their native land :
With me in dreadful harmony they join,
And weave with bloody hands the tissue of thy line.

' Weave the warp, and weave the woof
 The winding-sheet of Edward's race.
Give ample room, and verge enough
 The characters of hell to trace.
Mark the year, and mark the night,
When Severn shall re-echo with affright
The shrieks of death, thro' Berkley's roofs that ring,
Shrieks of an agonising king !
 She-wolf of France, with unrelenting fangs,
That tear'st the bowels of thy mangled Mate,
 From thee be born, who o'er thy country hangs
The scourge of Heaven ! What terrors round him wait
Amazement in his van, with Flight combined,
And Sorrow's faded form, and Solitude behind.

' Mighty victor, mighty Lord !
 Low on his funeral couch he lies !
No pitying heart, no eye, afford
 A tear to grace his obsequies.

Is the sable warriour fled?
Thy son is gone.   He rests among the Dead.
The Swarm that in thy noon-tide beam were born?
Gone to salute the rising Morn.
Fair laughs the Morn, and soft the Zephyr blows,
  While proudly riding o'er the azure realm
In gallant trim the gilded Vessel goes;
  Youth on the prow, and Pleasure at the helm;
Regardless of the sweeping Whirlwind's sway,
  That hush'd in grim repose expects his evening-prey.

  ' Fill high the sparkling bowl,
The rich repast prepare,
  Reft of a crown, he yet may share the feast:
Close by the regal chair
  Fell Thirst and Famine scowl
  A baleful smile upon their baffled Guest.
Heard ye the din of battle bray,
  Lance to lance, and horse to horse?
  Long years of havock urge their destined course,
And thro' the kindred squadrons mow their way.
  Ye towers of Julius, London's lasting shame,
With many a foul and midnight murther fed,
  Revere his Consort's faith, his Father's fame,
And spare the meek Usurper's holy head.
Above, below, the rose of snow,
  Twined with her blushing foe, we spread:
The bristled Boar in infant-gore
  Wallows beneath the thorny shade.
Now, Brothers, bending o'er the accursèd loom,
Stamp we our vengeance deep, and ratify his doom.

' Edward, lo! to sudden fate
  (Weave we the woof.   The thread is spun.)
Half of thy heart we consecrate.
  (The web is wove.   The work is done.)
Stay, O stay! nor thus forlorn
Leave me unbless'd, unpitied, here to mourn:
In yon bright track, that fires the western skies,
They melt, they vanish from my eyes.

But oh! what solemn scenes on Snowdon's height
  Descending slow their glitt'ring skirts unroll?
Visions of glory, spare my aching sight,
  Ye unborn Ages, crowd not on my soul!
No more our long-lost Arthur we bewail :—
All hail, ye genuine kings! Britannia's issue, hail!

' Girt with many a baron bold
Sublime their starry fronts they rear;
  And gorgeous Dames, and Statesmen old
In bearded majesty, appear.
In the midst a form divine!
Her eye proclaims her of the Briton-Line:
Her lyon-port, her awe-commanding face
Attemper'd sweet to virgin-grace.
What strings symphonious tremble in the air,
  What strains of vocal transport round her play.
Hear from the grave, great Taliessin, hear;
  They breathe a soul to animate thy clay.
Bright Rapture calls, and soaring, as she sings,
Waves in the eye of Heav'n her many-colour'd wings.

' The verse adorn again
  Fierce War, and faithful Love,
And Truth severe, by fairy Fiction drest.
  In buskin'd measures move
Pale Grief, and pleasing Pain,
With Horrour, Tyrant of the throbbing breast.
A voice as of the Cherub-Choir
  Gales from blooming Eden bear;
  And distant warblings lessen on my ear,
That lost in long futurity expire.
Fond impious Man, think'st thou, yon sanguine cloud
  Raised by thy breath, has quench'd the orb of day?
To-morrow he repairs the golden flood,
  And warms the nations with redoubled ray.
Enough for me: with joy I see
  The different doom our fates assign:
Be thine Despair and sceptred Care,
  To triumph, and to die, are mine.'
—He spoke, and headlong from the mountain's height
Deep in the roaring tide he plunged to endless night.

T. Gray.

SONG

WHERE shall the lover rest,
  Whom the fates sever
From his true maiden's breast,
  Parted for ever ?
Where, through groves deep and high,
  Sounds the far billow,
Where early violets die,
  Under the willow.

CHORUS

Eleu loro, &c.   Soft shall be his pillow.

There, through the summer day,
  Cool streams are laving ;
There, while the tempests sway,
  Scarce are boughs waving ;
There, thy rest shalt thou take,
  Parted for ever,
Never again to wake,
  Never, O never !

CHORUS

Eleu loro, &c.   Never, O never !

Where shall the traitor rest,
  He, the deceiver,
Who could win maiden's breast,
  Ruin, and leave her ?
In the lost battle,
  Borne down by the flying,
Where mingles war's rattle
  With groans of the dying.

CHORUS

Eleu loro, &c.   There shall he be lying.

Her wing shall the eagle flap
   O'er the false-hearted ;
His warm blood the wolf shall lap,
   Ere life be parted.
Shame and dishonour sit
   By his grave ever ;
Blessing shall hallow it,—
   Never, O never !

CHORUS

Eleu loro, &c.   Never, O never !

SIR W. SCOTT.

KINMONT WILLIE

O HAVE ye na heard o' the fause Sakelde ?
   O have ye na heard o' the keen Lord Scroope ?
How they hae ta'en bauld Kinmont Willie,
   On Hairibee to hang him up ?

Had Willie had but twenty men,
   But twenty men as stout as he,
Fause Sakelde had never the Kinmont ta'en,
   Wi' eight score in his cumpanie.

They band his legs beneath the steed,
   They tied his hands behind his back ;
They guarded him, fivesome on each side,
   And they brought him ower the Liddel-rack.

They led him thro' the Liddel-rack,
   And also thro' the Carlisle sands ;
They brought him on to Carlisle castell,
   To be at my Lord Scroope's commands.

' My hands are tied, but my tongue is free,
   And whae will dare this deed avow ?
Or answer by the Border law ?
   Or answer to the bauld Buccleuch ? '

' Now haud thy tongue, thou rank reiver !
   There's never a Scot shall set ye free :
Before ye cross my castle yate,
   I trow ye shall take farewell o' me.'

' Fear na ye that, my lord,' quo' Willie :
   ' By the faith o' my body, Lord Scroope,' he said,
I never yet lodged in a hostelrie,
   But I paid my lawing before I gaed.'

Now word is gane to the bauld Keeper,
   In Branksome Ha' where that he lay,
That Lord Scroope has ta'en the Kinmont Willie,
   Between the hours of night and day.

He has ta'en the table wi' his hand,
   He garr'd the red wine spring on hie—
' Now Christ's curse on my head,' he said,
   ' But avengèd of Lord Scroope I'll be !

' O is my basnet a widow's curch ?
   Or my lance a wand of the willow tree ?
Or my arm a lady's lilye hand,
   That an English lord should lightly me !

' And have they ta'en him, Kinmont Willie,
   Against the truce of Border tide ?
And forgotten that the bauld Buccleuch
   Is Keeper here on the Scottish side ?

' And have they e'en ta'en him, Kinmont Willie,
   Withouten either dread or fear ?
And forgotten that the bauld Buccleuch
   Can back a steed, or shake a spear ?

' O were there war between the lands,
    As well I wot that there is none,
I would slight Carlisle castell high,
    Tho' it were builded of marble stone.

' I would set that castell in a low,
    And sloken it with English blood !
There's nevir a man in Cumberland
    Should ken where Carlisle castell stood.

' But since nae war's between the lands,
    And there is peace, and peace should be ;
I'll neither harm English lad or lass,
    And yet the Kinmont freed shall be ! '

He has call'd him forty marchmen bauld,
    I trow they were of his ain name,
Except Sir Gilbert Elliot, call'd
    The laird of Stobs, I mean the same.

He has call'd him forty marchmen bauld,
    Were kinsmen to the bauld Buccleuch ;
With spur on heel, and splent on spauld,
    And gleuves of green, and feathers blue.

There were five and five before them a',
    Wi' hunting-horns and bugles bright ;
And five and five came wi' Buccleuch,
    Like warden's men, arrayed for fight.

And five and five, like a mason gang,
    That carried the ladders lang and hie ;
And five and five, like broken men ;
    And so they reached the Woodhouselee.

And as we cross'd the Bateable Land,
    When to the English side we held,
The first o' men that we met wi',
    Whae sould it be but fause Sakelde ?

'Where be ye gaun, ye hunters keen?'
  Quo' fause Sakelde; 'come tell to me!'
'We go to hunt an English stag,
  Has trespass'd on the Scots countrie.

'Where be ye gaun, ye marshal men?'
  Quo' fause Sakelde; 'come tell me true!
'We go to catch a rank reiver,
  Has broken faith wi' the bauld Buccleuch.'

'Where are ye gaun, ye mason lads,
  Wi' a' your ladders, lang and hie?'
'We gang to herry a corbie's nest,
  That wons not far frae Woodhouselee.'

'Where be ye gaun ye broken men?'
  Quo' fause Sakelde; 'come tell to me!'
Now Dickie of Dryhope led that band,
  And the never a word o' lear had he.

'Why trespass ye on the English side?
  Row-footed outlaws, stand!' quo' he;
The nevir a word had Dickie to say,
  Sae he thrust the lance through his fause bodie.

Then on we held for Carlisle toun,
  And at Staneshaw-bank the Eden we cross'd;
The water was great and meikle of spait,
  But the niver a horse nor man we lost.

And when we reach'd the Staneshaw-bank,
  The wind was rising loud and hie;
And there the laird garr'd leave our steeds,
  For fear that they should stamp and nie.

And when we left the Staneshaw-bank,
  The wind began full loud to blaw;
But 'twas wind and weet, and fire and sleet,
  When we came beneath the castle wa'.

We crept on knees, and held our breath,
　　Till we placed the ladders against the wa';
And sae ready was Buccleuch himsell
　　To mount the first, before us a'.

He has ta'en the watchman by the throat,
　　He flung him down upon the lead—
'Had there not been peace between our lands,
　　Upon the other side thou hadst gaed!

'Now sound out, trumpets!' quo' Buccleuch;
　　'Let's waken Lord Scroope right merrilie!'
Then loud the warden's trumpet blew—
　　'*O wha dare meddle wi' me?*'

Then speedilie to work we gaed,
 And raised the slogan ane and a',
And cut a hole thro' a sheet of lead,
 And so we wan to the castle ha'.

They thought King James and a' his men
 Had won the house wi' bow and spear;
It was but twenty Scots and ten,
 That put a thousand in sic a stear!

Wi' coulters, and wi' fore-hammers,
 We garr'd the bars bang merrilie,
Until we cam to the inner prison,
 Where Willie o' Kinmont he did lie.

And when we cam to the lower prison,
 Where Willie o' Kinmont he did lie—
' O sleep ye, wake ye, Kinmont Willie,
 Upon the morn that thou's to die?'

' O I sleep saft, and I wake aft;
 It's lang since sleeping was fley'd frae me;
Gie my service back to my wife and bairns,
 And a' gude fellows that spier for me.'

Then Red Rowan has hente him up,
 The starkest man in Teviotdale—
' Abide, abide now, Red Rowan,
 Till of my Lord Scroope I take farewell.

' Farewell, farewell, my gude Lord Scroope!
 My gude Lord Scroope, farewell!' he cried—
' I'll pay you for my lodging maill,
 When first we meet on the Border side.'

Then shoulder high, with shout and cry,
 We bore him down the ladder lang;
At every stride Red Rowan made,
 I wot the Kinmont's airns played clang!

' O mony a time,' quo' Kinmont Willie,
  ' I have ridden horse baith wild and wood;
But a rougher beast than Red Rowan,
  I ween my legs have ne'er bestrode.

'And mony a time,' quo' Kinmont Willie,
  ' I've pricked a horse out oure the furs;
But since the day I backed a steed,
  I never wore sic cumbrous spurs! '

We scarce had won the Staneshaw-bank,
  When a' the Carlisle bells were rung,
And a thousand men, in horse and foot,
  Cam' wi' the keen Lord Scroope along.

Buccleuch has turned to Eden water,
  Even where it flow'd frae bank to brim,
And he has plunged in wi' a' his band,
  And safely swam them thro' the stream.

He turned him on the other side,
  And at Lord Scroope his glove flung he—
' If ye like na my visit in merry England,
  In fair Scotland come visit me! '

All sore astonished stood Lord Scroope,
  He stood as still as rock of stane;
He scarcely dared to trew his eyes,
  When thro' the water they had gane.

' He is either himsell a devil frae hell,
  Or else his mother a witch maun be;
I wadna have ridden that wan water
  For a' the gowd in Christentie.'

Minstrelsy of the Scottish Border.

THE LAST MAN

ALL worldly shapes shall melt in gloom,
　The Sun himself must die,
Before this mortal shall assume
　Its Immortality!
I saw a vision in my sleep,
That gave my spirit strength to sweep
　Adown the gulph of Time!
I saw the last of human mould,
That shall Creation's death behold,
　As Adam saw her prime!

The Sun's eye had a sickly glare,
　The Earth with age was wan,
The skeletons of nations were
　Around that lonely man!
Some had expired in fight,—the brands
Still rested in their bony hands;
　In plague and famine some!
Earth's cities had no sound nor tread;
And ships were drifting with the dead
　To shores where all was dumb!

Yet, prophet-like, that lone one stood
　With dauntless words and high,
That shook the sere leaves from the wood
　As if a storm passed by,
Saying, 'We are twins in death, proud Sun!
Thy face is cold, thy race is run,
　'Tis Mercy bids thee go;
For thou ten thousand thousand years
Hast seen the tide of human tears,
　That shall no longer flow.

'What though beneath thee man put forth
　His pomp, his pride, his skill;
And arts that made fire, flood, and earth,
　The vassals of his will;—

Yet mourn I not thy parted sway,
Thou dim discrownèd king of day :
　　For all those trophied arts
And triumphs that beneath thee sprang,
Heal'd not a passion or a pang
　　Entail'd on human hearts.

' Go, let oblivion's curtain fall
　　Upon the stage of men,
Nor with thy rising beams recall
　　Life's tragedy again :
Its piteous pageants bring not back,
Nor waken flesh, upon the rack
　　Of pain anew to writhe ;
Stretch'd in disease's shapes abhorr'd,
Or mown in battle by the sword,
　　Like grass beneath the scythe.

' E'en I am weary in yon skies
　　To watch thy fading fire ;
Test of all sumless agonies,
　　Behold not me expire.
My lips that speak thy dirge of death—
Their rounded gasp and gurgling breath
　　To see thou shalt not boast.
The eclipse of Nature spreads my pall,—
The majesty of Darkness shall
　　Receive my parting ghost !

' This spirit shall return to Him
　　That gave its heavenly spark ;
Yet think not, Sun, it shall be dim
　　When thou thyself art dark !
No ! it shall live again, and shine
In bliss unknown to beams of thine,
　　By Him recalled to breath,
Who captive led captivity,
Who robb'd the grave of Victory,—
　　And took the sting from Death !

Go, Sun, while Mercy holds me up
   On Nature's awful waste
To drink this last and bitter cup
   Of grief that man shall taste—
Go, tell the night that hides thy face,
Thou saw'st the last of Adam's race,
   On Earth's sepulchral clod,
The darkening universe defy
To quench his Immortality,
   Or shake his trust in God!'

                   T. CAMPBELL.

IVRY

A SONG OF THE HUGUENOTS

Now glory to the Lord of Hosts, from whom all glories are!
And glory to our Sovereign Liege, King Henry of Navarre!
Now let there be the merry sound of music and of dance,
   Through thy corn-fields green, and sunny vines, oh pleasant land of
       France!
And thou, Rochelle, our own Rochelle, proud city of the waters,
Again let rapture light the eyes of all thy mourning daughters.
As thou wert constant in our ills, be joyous in our joy,
For cold, and stiff, and still are they who wrought thy walls annoy
Hurrah! Hurrah! a single field hath turned the chance of war,
Hurrah! Hurrah! for Ivry, and Henry of Navarre.

Oh! how our hearts were beating, when, at the dawn of day,
We saw the army of the League drawn out in long array;
With all its priest-led citizens, and all its rebel peers,
And Appenzel's stout infantry, and Egmont's Flemish spears.
There rode the brood of false Lorraine, the curses of our land;
And dark Mayenne was in the midst, a truncheon in his hand:
And, as we looked on them, we thought of Seine's empurpled
       flood,
And good Coligni's hoary hair all dabbled with his blood;
And we cried unto the living God, who rules the fate of war,
To fight for His own holy name, and Henry of Navarre.

S

The King is come to marshal us, in all his armour drest,
And he has bound a snow-white plume upon his gallant crest.
He looked upon his people, and a tear was in his eye ;
He looked upon the traitors, and his glance was stern and high.
Right graciously he smiled on us, as rolled from wing to wing,
Down all our line, a deafening shout, 'God save our Lord the
　　　　King ! '
' And if my standard-bearer fall, as fall full well he may,
For never saw I promise yet of such a bloody fray,
Press where ye see my white plume shine, amidst the ranks of war,
And be your oriflamme to-day the helmet of Navarre.'

Hurrah ! the foes are moving.　Hark to the mingled din,
Of fife, and steed, and trump, and drum, and roaring culverin.
The fiery Duke is pricking fast across Saint André's plain,
With all the hireling chivalry of Guelders and Almayne.
Now by the lips of those ye love, fair gentlemen of France,
Charge for the golden lilies,—upon them with the lance.
A thousand spurs are striking deep, a thousand spears in rest,
A thousand knights are pressing close behind the snow-white crest ;
And in they burst, and on they rushed, while like a guiding star,
Amidst the thickest carnage blazed the helmet of Navarre.

Now, God be praised, the day is ours.　Mayenne hath turned his
　　　　rein.
D'Aumale hath cried for quarter.　The Flemish count is slain.
Their ranks are breaking like thin clouds before a Biscay gale ;
The field is heaped with bleeding steeds, and flags, and cloven mail.
And then we thought on vengeance, and, all along our van,
' Remember St. Bartholomew,' was passed from man to man.
But out spake gentle Henry, ' No Frenchman is my foe :
Down, down with every foreigner, but let your brethren go.'
Oh ! was there ever such a knight in friendship or in war,
As our Sovereign Lord, King Henry, the soldier of Navarre ?

Right well fought all the Frenchmen who fought for France to-day ;
And many a lordly banner God gave them for a prey.
But we of the religion have borne us best in fight ;
And the good Lord of Rosny has ta'en the cornet white.
Our own true Maximilian the cornet white hath ta'en,
The cornet white with crosses black, the flag of false Lorraine.

Up with it high ; unfurl it wide ; that all the host may know
How God hath humbled the proud house which wrought His
 Church such woe.
Then on the ground, while trumpets sound their loudest point of
 war,
Fling the red shreds, a footcloth meet for Henry of Navarre.

Ho ! maidens of Vienna ; Ho ! matrons of Lucerne ;
Weep, weep, and rend your hair for those who never shall return.
Ho ! Philip, send, for charity, thy Mexican pistoles,
That Antwerp monks may sing a mass for thy poor spearmen's
 souls.
Ho ! gallant nobles of the League, look that your arms be bright ;
Ho ! burghers of Saint Genevieve, keep watch and ward to-night.
For our God hath crushed the tyrant, our God hath raised the
 slave,
And mocked the counsel of the wise, and the valour of the brave.
Then glory to His holy name, from whom all glories are ;
And glory to our Sovereign Lord, King Henry of Navarre.

LORD MACAULAY.

SIR PATRICK SPENS

THE king sits in Dunfermline toun,
 Drinking the blude-red wine :
' O whare will I get a skeely skipper
 To sail this new ship of mine ? '

O up and spake an eldern knight,
 Sat at the king's right knee—
' Sir Patrick Spens is the best sailor
 That ever sailed the sea.'

Our king has written a braid letter,
 And sealed it with his hand,
And sent it to Sir Patrick Spens,
 Was walking on the strand.

‘ To Noroway, to Noroway,
    To Noroway o’er the faem ;
The king’s daughter of Noroway,
    ’Tis thou maun bring her hame.’

The first word that Sir Patrick read,
    Sae loud loud laughed he ;
The neist word that Sir Patrick read,
    The tear blinded his e’e.

' O wha is this has done this deed,
  And tauld the king o' me,
To send us out, at this time of the year,
  To sail upon the sea ? '

' Be it wind, be it weet, be it hail, be it sleet,
  Our ship must sail the faem ;
The king's daughter of Noroway,
  'Tis we must fetch her hame.'

They hoysed their sails on Monenday morn,
  Wi' a' the speed they may ;
And they hae landed in Noroway
  Upon a Wedensday.

They hadna been a week, a week
  In Noroway but twae,
When that the lords o' Noroway
  Began aloud to say:

' Ye Scottishmen spend a' our king's gowd,
  And a' our queenis fee.'
' Ye lie, ye lie, ye liars loud !
  Fu' loud I hear ye lie !

' For I hae brought as much white monie
  As gane my men and me—
And I hae brought a half-fou' o' gude red gowd
  Out o'er the sea wi' me.

' Make ready, make ready, my merry men a' !
  Our gude ship sails the morn.'
' Now ever alake, my master dear,
  I fear a deadly storm !

' I saw the new moon, late yestreen,
  Wi' the auld moon in her arm ;
And if we gang to sea, master,
  I fear we'll come to harm.'

They hadna sail'd a league, a league,
   A league but barely three,
When the lift grew dark, and the wind blew loud,
   And gurly grew the sea.

The ankers brak, and the top-masts lap,
   It was sic a deadly storm;
And the waves cam' o'er the broken ship
   Till a' her sides were torn.

' O where will I get a gude sailor,
   To take my helm in hand,
Till I get up to the tall top-mast;
   To see if I can spy land ? '

' O here am I, a sailor gude,
   To take the helm in hand,
Till ye get up to the tall top-mast:
   But I fear you'll ne'er spy land.'

He hadna gane a step, a step,
   A step but barely ane,
When a bout flew out of our goodly ship,
   And the salt sea it came in.

' Gae, fetch a web o' the silken claith,
   Another o' the twine,
And wap them into our ship's side,
   And letna the sea come in.'

They fetch'd a web o' the silken claith,
   Another o' the twine,
And they wapped them round that gude ship's side,
   But still the sea came in.

O laith laith were our gude Scots lords
   To wet their cork-heeled shoon !
But lang ere a' the play was play'd
   They wat their hats aboon.

And mony was the feather-bed
   That floated on the faem,
And mony was the gude lord's son
   That never mair came hame.

The ladyes wrang their fingers white—
  The maidens tore their hair;
A' for the sake of their true loves—
  For them they'll see na mair.

O lang lang may the ladyes sit,
  Wi' their fans into their hand,
Before they see Sir Patrick Spens
  Come sailing to the strand!

And lang lang may the maidens sit,
　Wi' the goud kaims in their hair,
A' waiting for their ain dear loves—
　For them they'll see na mair.

O forty miles off Aberdour,
　'Tis fifty fathoms deep,
And there lies gude Sir Patrick Spens,
　Wi' the Scots lords at his feet.

LA BELLE DAME SANS MERCY

Ah! what can ail thee, wretched wight,
　Alone and palely loitering?
The sedge is withered from the lake,
　And no birds sing.

Ah! what can ail thee, wretched wight,
　So haggard and so woe-begone?
The squirrel's granary is full,
　And the harvest's done.

I see a lily on thy brow,
　With anguish moist and fever-dew;
And on thy cheek a fading rose
　Fast withereth too.

I met a lady in the meads,
　Full beautiful—a fairy's child;
Her hair was long, her foot was light,
　And her eyes were wild.

I set her on my pacing steed,
　And nothing else saw all day long;
For sideways would she lean and sing
　A fairy's song.

AND NOTHING ELSE SAW ALL DAY LONG.

I made a garland for her head,
　　And bracelets too, and fragrant zone;
She looked at me as she did love,
　　And made sweet moan.

She found me roots of relish sweet,
　　And honey wild, and manna-dew;
And sure in language strange she said,
　　I love thee true.

She took me to her elfin grot,
　　And there she gazèd and sighèd deep,
And there I shut her wild sad eyes—
　　So kissed to sleep.

And there we slumbered on the moss,
　　And there I dreamed, ah! woe betide,
The latest dream I ever dreamed,
　　On the cold hill-side.

I saw pale kings and princes too,
　　Pale warriors—death-pale were they all;
Who cried, ' La Belle Dame Sans Mercy
　　Hath thee in thrall ! '

I saw their starved lips in the gloom,
　　With horrid warning gapèd wide;
And I awoke, and found me here
　　On the cold hill-side.

And this is why I sojourn here,
　　Alone and palely loitering:
Though the sedge is withered from the lake,
　　And no birds sing.

J. KEATS.

THE CHILD AND THE SNAKE

HENRY was every morning fed
With a full mess of milk and bread.
One day the boy his breakfast took,
And ate it by a purling brook.
Which through his mother's orchard ran.
From that time ever when he can
Escape his mother's eye, he there
Takes his food in th' open air.
Finding the child delight to eat
Abroad, and make the grass his seat,
His mother lets him have his way.
With free leave Henry every day
Thither repairs, until she heard
Him talking of a fine *grey bird.*
This pretty bird, he said, indeed,
Came every day with him to feed,
And it loved him and loved his milk,
And it was smooth and soft like silk.
His mother thought she'd go and see
What sort of bird this same might be.
So the next morn she follows Harry,
And carefully she sees him carry
Through the long grass his heap'd-up mess.
What was her terror and distress,
When she saw the infant take
His bread and milk close to a snake!
Upon the grass he spreads his feast,
And sits down by his frightful guest,
Who had waited for the treat;
And now they both began to eat.
Fond mother! shriek not, O beware
The least small noise, O have a care—
The least small noise that may be made,
The wily snake will be afraid—
If he hear the lightest sound,
He will inflict th' envenom'd wound.

—She speaks not, moves not, scarce does breathe,
As she stands the trees beneath ;
No sound she utters ; and she soon
Sees the child lift up his spoon,
And tap the snake upon the head,
Fearless of harm ; and then he said,

As speaking to familiar mate,
' Keep on your own side, do, Grey Pate : '
The snake then to the other side,
As one rebukèd, seems to glide ;
And now again advancing nigh,
Again she hears the infant cry,

Tapping the snake, ' Keep further, do ;
' Mind, Grey Pate, what I say to you.'
The danger's o'er—she sees the boy
(O what a change from fear to joy !)
Rise and bid the snake ' Good-bye ; '
Says he, ' Our breakfast's done, and I
' Will come again to-morrow day ; '
—Then, lightly tripping, ran away.

M. Lamb.

TOM BOWLING

Here, a sheer hulk, lies poor Tom Bowling,
   The darling of our crew,
No more he'll hear the tempest howling,
   For death has broach'd him to.
His form was of the manliest beauty,
   His heart was kind and soft,
Faithful below he did his duty ;
   But now he's gone aloft.

Tom never from his word departed,
   His virtues were so rare,
His friends were many and true-hearted,
   His Poll was kind and fair :
And then he'd sing so blithe and jolly,
   Ah, many's the time and oft !
But mirth is turn'd to melancholy,
   For Tom is gone aloft.

Yet shall poor Tom find pleasant weather,
   When He who all commands,
Shall give, to call life's crew together,
   The word to pipe all hands.
Thus Death, who kings and tars despatches,
   In vain Tom's life has doff'd ;
For though his body's under hatches,
   His soul has gone aloft.

C. Dibdin.

THE KITTEN AND FALLING LEAVES

THAT way look, my Infant, lo!
What a pretty baby-show!
See the Kitten on the wall,
Sporting with the leaves that fall,
Withered leaves—one—two—and three—
From the lofty elder-tree!
Through the calm and frosty air
Of this morning bright and fair,
Eddying round and round they sink
Softly, slowly: one might think,
From the motions that are made,
Every little leaf conveyed
Sylph or Faery hither tending,—
To this lower world descending,
Each invisible and mute,
In his wavering parachute.
——But the Kitten, how she starts,
Crouches, stretches, paws, and darts!
First at one, and then its fellow,
Just as light and just as yellow;
There are many now—now one—
Now they stop, and there are none:
What intenseness of desire
In her upward eye of fire!
With a tiger-leap half way
Now she meets the coming prey,
Lets it go as fast, and then
Has it in her power again:
Now she works with three or four,
Like an Indian conjuror;
Quick as he in feats of art,
Far beyond in joy of heart.
Were her antics played in th' eye
Of a thousand standers-by,
Clapping hands with shout and stare,
What would little Tabby care

For the plaudits of the crowd?
Over happy to be proud,
Over wealthy in the treasure
Of her own exceeding pleasure!

'Tis a pretty baby-treat;
Nor, I deem, for me unmeet;
Here, for neither Babe nor me,
Other play-mate can I see.
Of the countless living things,
That with stir of feet and wings
(In the sun or under shade,
Upon bough or grassy blade)
And with busy revellings,
Chirp and song, and murmurings,
Made this orchard's narrow space
And this vale so blithe a place,
Multitudes are swept away
Never more to breathe the day:
Some are sleeping; some in bands
Travelled into distant lands;
Others slunk to moor and wood,
Far from human neighbourhood;
And, among the Kinds that keep
With us closer fellowship,
With us openly abide,
All have laid their mirth aside.
Where is he that giddy Sprite,
Blue-cap, with his colours bright,
Who was blest as bird could be,
Feeding in the apple-tree;
Made such wanton spoil and rout,
Turning blossoms inside out;
Hung—head pointing towards the ground—
Fluttered, perched, into a round
Bound himself, and then unbound;
Lithest, gaudiest Harlequin!
Prettiest Tumbler ever seen!
Light of heart and light of limb;
What is now become of Him?

Lambs, that through the mountains went
Frisking, bleating merriment,
When the year was in its prime,
They are sobered by this time.
If you look to vale or hill,
If you listen, all is still,
Save a little neighbouring rill,
That from out the rocky ground
Strikes a solitary sound.
Vainly glitter hill and plain,
And the air is calm in vain;
Vainly Morning spreads the lure
Of a sky serene and pure;
Creature none can she decoy
Into open sign of joy:
Is it that they have a fear
Of the dreary season near?
Or that other pleasures be
Sweeter even than gaiety?
   Yet, whate'er enjoyments dwell
In the impenetrable cell
Of the silent heart which Nature
Furnishes to every creature;
Whatso'er we feel and know
Too sedate for outward show,
Such a light of gladness breaks,
Pretty Kitten! from thy freaks,
Spreads with such a living grace
O'er my little Dora's face;
Yes, the sight so stirs and charms
Thee, Baby, laughing in my arms,
That almost I could repine
That your transports are not mine,
That I do not wholly fare
Even as ye do, thoughtless pair!
And I will have my careless season,
Spite of melancholy reason,
Will walk through life in such a way
That, when time brings on decay,
Now and then I may possess
Hours of perfect gladsomeness.

T

—Pleased by any random toy;
By a kitten's busy joy,
Or an infant's laughing eye
Sharing in the ecstasy;
I would fare like that or this,
Find my wisdom in my bliss;
Keep the sprightly soul awake;
And have faculties to take,
Even from things by sorrow wrought
Matter for a jocund thought;
Spite of care, and spite of grief,
To gambol with Life's falling Leaf.

W. WORDSWORTH.

THE PILGRIM

WHO would true valour see
　　Let him come hither!
One here will constant be,
　　Come wind, come weather:
There's no discouragement
Shall make him once relent
His first-avow'd intent
　　To be a Pilgrim.

Whoso beset him round
　　With dismal stories,
Do but themselves confound;
　　His strength the more is.
No lion can him fright;
He'll with a giant fight;
But he will have a right
　　To be a Pilgrim.

Nor enemy, nor fiend,
　　Can daunt his spirit;
He knows he at the end
　　Shall Life inherit:—

Then, fancies, fly away;
He'll not fear what men say;
He'll labour, night and day
　　To be a Pilgrim.

J. BUNYAN.

T 2

THE SOLITUDE OF ALEXANDER SELKIRK

I AM monarch of all I survey,
  My right there is none to dispute,
From the centre all round to the sea,
  I am lord of the fowl and the brute.
O Solitude! where are the charms
  That sages have seen in thy face?
Better dwell in the midst of alarms,
  Than reign in this horrible place.

I am out of humanity's reach,
  I must finish my journey alone,
Never hear the sweet music of speech,—
  I start at the sound of my own.
The beasts that roam over the plain
  My form with indifference see;
They are so unacquainted with man,
  Their tameness is shocking to me.

Society, Friendship, and Love,
  Divinely bestow'd upon man,
Oh, had I the wings of a dove
  How soon would I taste you again!
My sorrows I then might assuage
  In the ways of religion and truth,
Might learn from the wisdom of age,
  And be cheer'd by the sallies of youth.

Ye winds that have made me your sport,
  Convey to this desolate shore
Some cordial endearing report
  Of a land I shall visit no more!
My friends, do they now and then send
  A wish or a thought after me?
Oh, tell me I yet have a friend,
  Though a friend I am never to see.

How fleet is a glance of the mind!
    Compared with the speed of its flight,
The tempest itself lags behind,
    And the swift-wingèd arrows of light.

When I think of my own native land,
    In a moment I seem to be there;
But alas! recollection at hand
    Soon hurries me back to despair.

—But the seafowl is gone to her nest,
 The beast is laid down in his lair,
Even here is a season of rest,
 And I to my cabin repair.
There's mercy in every place,
 And mercy, encouraging thought !
Gives even affliction a grace,
 And reconciles man to his lot.

W. COWPER.

THE EVE OF ST. JOHN

THE Baron of Smaylho'me rose with day,
 He spurr'd his courser on,
Without stop or stay, down the rocky way,
 That leads to Brotherstone.

He went not with the bold Buccleuch,
 His banner broad to rear ;
He went not 'gainst the English yew,
 To lift the Scottish spear.

Yet his plate-jack [1] was braced, and his helmet was laced,
 And his vaunt-brace of proof he wore ;
At his saddle-gerthe was a good steel sperthe,
 Full ten pound weight and more.

The Baron return'd in three days' space,
 And his looks were sad and sour ;
And weary was his courser's pace,
 As he reach'd his rocky tower.

He came not from where Ancram Moor
 Ran red with English blood ;
Where the Douglas true, and the bold Buccleuch,
 'Gainst keen Lord Evers stood.

---

[1] The plate-jack is coat armour ; the vaunt-brace, or wam-brace, armour for the body ; the sperthe, a battle-axe.

Yet was his helmet hack'd and hew'd,
   His acton pierced and tore,
His axe and his dagger with blood imbrued,—
   But it was not English gore.

He lighted at the Chapellage,
   He held him close and still;
And he whistled thrice for his little foot-page,
   His name was English Will.

' Come thou hither, my little foot-page;
   Come hither to my knee;
Though thou art young, and tender of age,
   I think thou art true to me.

' Come, tell me all that thou hast seen,
   And look thou tell me true!
Since I from Smaylho'me tower have been,
   What did thy lady do?'

' My lady, each night, sought the lonely light,
   That burns on the wild Watchfold;
For, from height to height, the beacons bright
   Of the English foemen told.

' The bittern clamour'd from the moss,
   The wind blew loud and shrill;
Yet the craggy pathway she did cross
   To the eiry Beacon Hill.

' I watched her steps, and silent came
   Where she sat her on a stone;
No watchman stood by the dreary flame;
   It burned all alone.

' The second night I kept her in sight,
   Till to the fire she came,
And, by Mary's might! an Armed Knight
   Stood by the lonely flame.

'And many a word that warlike lord
  Did speak to my lady there ;
But the rain fell fast, and loud blew the blast
  And I heard not what they were.

'The third night there the sky was fair,
  And the mountain-blast was still,
As again I watch'd the secret pair,
  On the lonesome Beacon Hill.

'And I heard her name the midnight hour,
  And name this holy eve ;
And say, " Come this night to thy lady's bower ;
  Ask no bold Baron's leave.

'" He lifts his spear with the bold Buccleuch ;
  His lady is all alone ;
The door she'll undo, to her knight so true,
  On the eve of good St. John."

'" I cannot come ; I must not come ;
  I dare not come to thee ;
On the eve of St. John I must wander alone :
  In thy bower I may not be."

'" Now, out on thee, faint-hearted knight !
  Thou should'st not say me nay ;
For the eve is sweet, and when lovers meet,
  Is worth the whole summer's day.

'" And I'll chain the blood-hound, and the warder shall
    not sound,
  And rushes shall be strew'd on the stair ;
So, by the black rood-stone, and by holy St. John,
  I conjure thee, my love, to be there ! "

'" Though the blood-hound be mute, and the rush beneath
    my foot,
  And the warder his bugle should not blow,
Yet there sleepeth a priest in the chamber to the east,
  And my footstep he would know."

' " O fear not the priest, who sleepeth to the east!
 For to Dryburgh the way he has ta'en ;
And there to say mass, till three days do pass,
 For the soul of a knight that is slayne."—

' He turn'd him around, and grimly he frown'd ;
 Then he laugh'd right scornfully—
" He who says the mass-rite for the soul of that knight
 May as well say mass for me.

' " At the lone midnight hour, when bad spirits have power,
 In thy chamber will I be."
With that he was gone, and my lady left alone,
 And no more did I see.'—

Then changed, I trow, was that bold Baron's brow,
 From the dark to the blood-red high ;
' Now, tell me the mien of the knight thou hast seen,
 For, by Mary, he shall die ! '

' His arms shone full bright, in the beacon's red light ;
 His plume it was scarlet and blue ;
On his shield was a hound, in a silver leash bound,
 And his crest was a branch of the yew.'

' Thou liest, thou liest, thou little foot-page,
 Loud dost thou lie to me !
For that knight is cold, and low laid in the mould,
 All under the Eildon-tree.'

' Yet hear but my word, my noble lord !
 For I heard her name his name ;
And that lady bright, she called the knight
 Sir Richard of Coldinghame.'

The bold Baron's brow then changed, I trow,
 From high blood-red to pale—
' The grave is deep and dark—and the corpse is stiff
 and stark—
 So I may not trust thy tale.

' Where fair Tweed flows round holy Melrose,
  And Eildon slopes to the plain,
Full three nights ago, by some secret foe,
  That gay gallant was slain.

' The varying light deceived thy sight,
  And the wild winds drown'd the name ;
For the Dryburgh bells ring, and the white monks do sing,
  For Sir Richard of Coldinghame ! '

He pass'd the court-gate, and he oped the tower-grate,
  And he mounted the narrow stair,
To the bartizan seat, where, with maids that on her wait,
  He found his lady fair.

That lady sat in mournful mood ;
  Look'd over hill and vale ;
Over Tweed's fair flood, and Mertoun's wood,
  And all down Teviotdale.

' Now hail, now hail, thou lady bright ! '
  ' Now hail, thou Baron true !
What news, what news, from Ancram fight ?
  What news from the bold Buccleuch ? '

' The Ancram moor is red with gore,
  For many a southern fell ;
And Buccleuch has charged us, evermore,
  To watch our beacons well.'

The lady blush'd red, but nothing she said ;
  Nor added the Baron a word:
Then she stepp'd down the stair to her chamber fair,
  And so did her moody lord.

In sleep the lady mourn'd, and the Baron toss'd and turn'd,
  And oft to himself he said—
' The worms around him creep, and his bloody grave is
  deep . .
  It cannot give up the dead ! '—

It was near the ringing of matin-bell,
 The night was well nigh done,
When a heavy sleep on that Baron fell,
 On the eve of good St. John.

The lady look'd through the chamber fair,
 By the light of a dying flame ;
And she was aware of a knight stood there—
 Sir Richard of Coldinghame !

' Alas ! away, away ! ' she cried,
 For the holy Virgin's sake ! —
· Lady, I know who sleeps by thy side ;
 But, lady, he will not awake.

' By Eildon tree, for long nights three,
 In bloody grave have I lain ;
The mass and the death-prayer are said for me,
 But, lady, they are said in vain.

' By the Baron's brand, near Tweed's fair strand,
 Most foully slain, I fell ;
And my restless sprite on the beacon's height,
 For a space is doom'd to dwell.

' At our trysting-place, for a certain space,
 I must wander to and fro ;
But I had not had power to come to thy bower,
 Had'st thou not conjured me so.'—

Love master'd fear—her brow she cross'd ;
 ' How, Richard, hast thou sped ?
And art thou saved, or art thou lost ? '
 The Vision shook his head !

' Who spilleth life, shall forfeit life :
 So bid thy lord believe :
That lawless love is guilt above,
 This awful sign receive.'

He laid his left palm on an oaken beam;
　His right upon her hand:
The lady shrunk, and fainting sunk,
　For it scorch'd like a fiery brand.

The sable score, of fingers four,
　Remains on that board impress'd;
And for evermore that lady wore
　A covering on her wrist.

There is a nun in Dryburgh bower,
　Ne'er looks upon the sun:
There is a monk in Melrose tower,
　He speaketh word to none.

That nun, who ne'er beholds the day,
　That monk, who speaks to none—
That nun was Smaylho'me's Lady gay,
　That monk the bold Baron.

SIR W. SCOTT.

LEADER HAUGHS

SING Erlington and Cowdenknowes where Homes had ance com-
　manding,
And Drygrange with the milk-white ewes, 'twixt Tweed and Leader
　standing.
The bird that flees through Reedpath trees, and Gledswood banks
　ilk morrow,
May chant and sing sweet Leader Haughs, and bonny howms of
　Yarrow.
But Minstrel Burn cannot assuage his grief while life endureth,
To see the changes of this age that fleeting time procureth,
For mony a place stands in hard case, where blyth folk kenned nae
　sorrow,
With Homes that dwelt on Leader braes, and Scott that dwelt on
　Yarrow.

MINSTREL BURN.

EPITAPH ON A HARE

HERE lies, whom hound did ne'er pursue,
  Nor swifter greyhound follow,
Whose foot ne'er tainted morning dew,
  Nor ear heard huntsman's halloo;

Old Tiney, surliest of his kind,
  Who, nursed with tender care,
And to domestic bounds confined,
  Was still a wild Jack hare.

Though duly from my hand he took
  His pittance every night,
He did it with a jealous look,
  And, when he could, would bite.

His diet was of wheaten bread,
  And milk, and oats, and straw;
Thistles, or lettuces instead,
  With sand to scour his maw.

On twigs of hawthorn he regaled,
  On pippins' russet peel,
And, when his juicy salads failed,
  Sliced carrot pleased him well.

A Turkey carpet was his lawn,
  Whereon he loved to bound,
To skip and gambol like a fawn,
  And swing his rump around.

His frisking was at evening hours,
  For then he lost his fear,
But most before approaching showers,
  Or when a storm drew near.

Eight years and five round rolling moons
    He thus saw steal away,
Dozing out all his idle noons,
    And every night at play.

I kept him for his humour's sake,
    For he would oft beguile
My heart of thoughts that made it ache,
    And force me to a smile.

But now beneath his walnut shade
    He finds his long last home,
And waits, in snug concealment laid.
    Till gentler Puss shall come.

He, still more aged, feels the shocks
    From which no care can save,
And, partner once of Tiney's box,
    Must soon partake his grave.

                  W. COWPER.

BATTLE OF OTTERBOURNE

IT fell about the Lammas tide,
    When the muir-men win their hay,
The doughty Earl of Douglas rode
    Into England, to catch a prey.

He chose the Gordons and the Graemes,
    With them the Lindesays, light and gay;
But the Jardines wald not with him ride,
    And they rue it to this day.

And he has burn'd the dales of Tyne,
    And part of Bambrough shire:
And three good towers on Roxburgh fells,
    He left them all on fire.

And he march'd up to Newcastle,
  And rode it round about ;
' O wha's the lord of this castle,
  Or wha's the lady o't ? '

But up spake proud Lord Percy, then,
  And O but he spake hie !
' I am the lord of this castle,
  My wife's the lady gay ! '

' If thou'rt the lord of this castle,
  Sae weel it pleases me !
For, ere I cross the border fells,
  The tane of us sall die.'

He took a lang spear in his hand,
  Shod with the metal free,
And for to meet the Douglas there,
  He rode right furiouslie.

But O how pale his lady look'd,
  Frae aff the castle wa',
When down, before the Scottish spear,
  She saw proud Percy fa'.

' Had we twa been upon the green,
  And never an eye to see,
I wad hae had you, flesh and fell ;
  But your sword sall gae wi' mee.'

' But gae ye up to Otterbourne
  And wait there dayis three ;
And, if I come not ere three dayis end,
  A fause knight ca' ye me.'

' The Otterbourne's a bonnie burn ;
  'Tis pleasant there to be ;
But there is nought at Otterbourne,
  To feed my men and me.

' The deer rins wild on hill and dale,
  The birds fly wild from tree to tree ;
But there is neither bread nor kale,
  To fend [1] my men and me.

' Yet I will stay at Otterbourne,
  Where you sall welcome be ;
And, if ye come not at three dayis end,
  A fause lord I'll ca' thee.'

' Thither will I come,' proud Percy said,
  ' By the might of Our Ladye ! '—
' There will I bide thee,' said the Douglas,
  ' My trowth I plight to thee.'

They lighted high on Otterbourne,
  Upon the bent sae brown ;
They lighted high on Otterbourne,
  And threw their pallions down.

---

[1] *Fend*, ' support.'

And he that had a bonnie boy,
  Sent out his horse to grass ;
And he that had not a bonnie boy,
  His ain servant he was.

But up then spake a little page,
  Before the peep of dawn—
' O waken ye, waken ye, my good lord,
  For Percy's hard at hand.'

' Ye lie, ye lie, ye liar loud !
  Sae loud I hear ye lie :
For Percy had not men yestreen,
  To dight my men and me.

' But I hae dream'd a dreary dream,
  Beyond the Isle of Sky ;
I saw a dead man win a fight,
  And I think that man was I.'

He belted on his good braid sword,
  And to the field he ran ;
But he forgot the helmet good,
  That should have kept his brain.

When Percy wi' the Douglas met,
  I wat he was fu' fain !
They swakked their swords, till sair they swat,
  And the blood ran down like rain.

But Percy with his good braid sword,
  That could so sharply wound,
Has wounded Douglas on the brow,
  Till he fell to the ground.

Then he call'd on his little foot-page,
  And said—' Run speedilie,
And fetch my ain dear sister's son,
  Sir Hugh Montgomery.

U

‘ My nephew good,’ the Douglas said,
　‘ What recks the death of ane !
Last night I dream’d a dreary dream,
　And I ken the day’s thy ain.

‘ My wound is deep ; I fain would sleep ;
　Take thou the vanguard of the three,
And hide me by the braken bush,
　That grows on yonder lilye lee.

‘ O bury me by the braken bush,
　Beneath the blooming briar,
Let never living mortal ken,
　That ere a kindly Scot lies here.’

He lifted up that noble lord,
　Wi’ the saut tear in his e’e ;
He hid him in the braken bush,
　That his merrie men might not see.

The moon was clear, the day drew near,
　The spears in flinders flew,
But mony a gallant Englishman
　Ere day the Scotsmen slew.

The Gordons good, in English blood
　They steeped their hose and shoon ;
The Lindesays flew like fire about,
　Till all the fray was done.

The Percy and Montgomery met,
　That either of other were fain ;
They swakked swords, and they twa swat,
　And aye the blude ran down between.

‘ Yield thee, O yield thee, Percy ! ’ he said,
　‘ Or else I vow I’ll lay thee low ! ’
‘ Whom to shall I yield,’ said Earl Percy,
　‘ Now that I see it must be so ? ’

' Thou shalt not yield to lord nor loun,
　Nor yet shalt thou yield to me ;
But yield thee to the braken bush,
　That grows upon yon lilye lee !'

' I will not yield to a braken bush,
　Nor yet will I yield to a briar ;
But I would yield to Earl Douglas,
　Or Sir Hugh the Montgomery, if he were here.'

As soon as he knew it was Montgomery,
　He stuck his sword's point in the gronde ;
And the Montgomery was a courteous knight,
　And quickly took him by the honde.

This deed was done at Otterbourne,
　About the breaking of the day ;
Earl Douglas was buried at the braken bush,
　And the Percy led captive away.

．　　　．　　　．　　．　　　．　　　．　　　．　　　．

MINSTRELSY OF THE SCOTTISH BORDER.

LYCIDAS

ELEGY ON A FRIEND DROWNED IN THE IRISH CHANNEL

YET once more, O ye laurels, and once more,
Ye myrtles brown, with ivy never sere,
I come to pluck your berries harsh and crude,
And with forc'd fingers rude
Shatter your leaves before the mellowing year.
Bitter constraint, and sad occasion dear,
Compels me to disturb your season due :
For Lycidas is dead, dead ere his prime,
Young Lycidas, and hath not left his peer :
Who would not sing for Lycidas ? he knew
Himself to sing, and build the lofty rhime.
He must not float upon his watery bier
Unwept, and welter to the parching wind,
Without the meed of some melodious tear.

· Begin then, Sisters of the sacred well,
That from beneath the seat of Jove doth spring,
Begin, and somewhat loudly sweep the string.
Hence with denial vain and coy excuse,
So may some gentle Muse
With lucky words favour my destin'd urn;
And as he passes turn
And bid fair peace be to my sable shroud.

For we were nursed upon the self-same hill,
Fed the same flock by fountain, shade, and rill.
Together both, ere the high lawns appear'd
Under the opening eyelids of the morn,
We drove a field, and both together heard
What time the gray-fly winds her sultry horn,
Battening our flocks with the fresh dews of night,
Oft till the star, that rose, at evening, bright,
Toward heaven's descent had sloped his west'ring wheel
Meanwhile the rural ditties were not mute,
Temper'd to the oaten flute,
Rough Satyrs danc'd; and Fauns with cloven heel
From the glad sound would not be absent long,
And old Damoetas loved to hear our song.

But, O the heavy change, now thou art gone,
Now thou art gone, and never must return!
Thee, Shepherd, thee the woods, and desert caves
With wild thyme and the gadding vine o'ergrown,
And all their echoes mourn.
The willows and the hazel copses green,
Shall now no more be seen,
Fanning their joyous leaves to thy soft lays.
As killing as the canker to the rose,
Or taint-worm to the weanling herds that graze,
Or frost to flow'rs, that their gay wardrobe wear,
When first the white-thorn blows;
Such, Lycidas, thy loss to shepherds' ear.

Where were ye, Nymphs, when the remorseless deep
Clos'd o'er the head of your lov'd Lycidas?
For neither were ye playing on the steep,

Where your old bards, the famous Druids, lie,
Nor on the shaggy top of Mona high,
Nor yet where Deva spreads her wizard stream :
Ay me ! I fondly dream !

Had ye been there, for what could that have done ?
What could the Muse herself that Orpheus bore,
The Muse herself, for her enchanting son,
Whom universal nature did lament,
When by the rout that made the hideous roar,
His gory visage down the stream was sent,
Down the swift Hebrus to the Lesbian shore ?

Alas ! what boots it with incessant care
To tend the homely slighted shepherd's trade
And strictly meditate the thankless Muse ?
Were it not better done as others use,
To sport with Amaryllis in the shade,
Or with the tangles of Neaera's hair ?
Fame is the spur that the clear spirit doth raise
(That last infirmity of noble mind)
To scorn delights, and live laborious days ;
But the fair guerdon when we hope to find,
And think to burst out into sudden blaze.
Comes the blind Fury with th' abhorrèd shears
And slits the thin-spun life. ' But not the praise,'
Phoebus replied, and touch'd my trembling ears ;
' Fame is no plant that grows on mortal soil,
Nor in the glist'ring foil
Set off to th' world, nor in broad rumour lies ;
But lives and spreads aloft by those pure eyes,
And perfect witness of all-judging Jove ;
As he pronounces lastly on each deed,
Of so much fame in heav'n expect thy meed.'

O fountain Arethuse, and thou honour'd flood,
Smooth-sliding Mincius, crown'd with vocal reeds,
That strain I heard was of a higher mood :
But now my oat proceeds,
And listens to the herald of the sea
That came in Neptune's plea ;
He ask'd the waves, and ask'd the felon winds,
What hard mishap hath doom'd this gentle swain ?
And question'd every gust of rugged wings
That blows from off each beakèd promontory :
They knew not of his story,
And sage Hippotadès their answer brings,
That not a blast was from his dungeon stray'd,
The air was calm, and on the level brine
Sleek Panopè with all her sisters play'd.
It was that fatal and perfidious bark
Built in th' eclipse, and rigg'd with curses dark,
That sunk so low that sacred head of thine.

Next Camus, reverend sire, went footing slow,
His mantle hairy, and his bonnet sedge,
Inwrought with figures dim, and on the edge
Like to that sanguine flow'r inscribed with woe.
' Ah! who hath reft,' quoth he, ' my dearest pledge! '
Last came, and last did go,

The pilot of the Galilean lake;
Two massy keys he bore of metals twain,
(The golden opes, the iron shuts amain);
He shook his mitred locks, and stern bespake,
' How well could I have spared for thee, young swain,
Enow of such, as for their bellies' sake

Creep and intrude, and climb into the fold?
Of other care they little reckoning make
Than how to scramble at the shearers' feast,
And shove away the worthy bidden guest;
Blind mouths! that scarce themselves know how to hold
A sheep-hook, or have learn'd aught else the least
That to the faithful herdman's art belongs!
What recks it them? What need they? They are sped'
And when they list, their lean and flashy songs
Grate on their scrannel pipes of wretched straw;
The hungry sheep look up, and are not fed,
But swoln with wind and the rank mist they draw,
Rot inwardly, and foul contagion spread:
Besides what the grim wolf with privy paw
Daily devours apace, and nothing said;
But that two-handed engine at the door
Stands ready to smite once, and smite no more.'

Return, Alphèus, the dread voice is past,
That shrunk thy streams; return, Sicilian Muse,
And call the vales, and bid them hither cast
Their bells, and flow'rets of a thousand hues.
Ye valleys low, where the mild whispers use
Of shades, and wanton winds, and gushing brooks,
On whose fresh lap the swart star sparely looks:
Throw hither all your quaint enamell'd eyes
That on the green turf suck the honied showers
And purple all the ground with vernal flowers.
Bring the rathe primrose that forsaken dies,
The tufted crow-toe, and pale jessamine,
The white pink, and the pansy freak'd with jet,
The glowing violet,
The musk-rose, and the well-attir'd woodbine,
With cowslips wan that hang the pensive head,
And every flower that sad embroidery wears:
Bid amaranthus all his beauty shed,
And daffadillies fill their cups with tears,
To strew the laureate hearse where Lycid lies.
For so to interpose a little ease,
Let our frail thoughts dally with false surmise.
Ay me! whilst thee the shores, and sounding seas

Wash far away, where'er thy bones are hurl'd,
Whether beyond the stormy Hebrides,
Where thou perhaps under the whelming tide,
Visit'st the bottom of the monstrous world;
Or whether thou to our moist vows denied,

Sleep'st by the fable of Bellerus old,
Where the great Vision of the guarded mount
Looks towards Namancos and Bayona's hold;
Look homeward Angel now, and melt with ruth:
And, O ye dolphins, waft the hapless youth.

Weep no more, woeful shepherds, weep no more
For Lycidas, your sorrow, is not dead,
Sunk though he be beneath the watery floor
So sinks the day-star in the ocean bed,

And yet anon repairs his drooping head,
And tricks his beams, and with new spangled ore
Flames in the forehead of the morning sky:
So Lycidas sunk low, but mounted high,
Through the dear might of Him that walk'd the waves,
Where other groves, and other streams along,
With nectar pure his oozy locks he laves,
And hears the unexpressive nuptial song
In the blest kingdoms meek of joy and love.
There entertain him all the saints above,
In solemn troops, and sweet societies,
That sing, and singing, in their glory move,
And wipe the tears for ever from his eyes.
Now, Lycidas, the shepherds weep no more;
Henceforth thou art the Genius of the shore,
In thy large recompense, and shalt be good
To all that wander in that perilous flood.

Thus sang the uncouth swain to th' oaks and rills,
While the still morn went out with sandals gray,
He touch'd the tender stops of various quills,
With eager thought warbling his Doric lay;
And now the sun had stretch'd out all the hills,
And now was dropt into the western bay:
At last he rose, and twitch'd his mantle blue;
To-morrow to fresh woods, and pastures new.

                                        J. MILTON.

ELEGY WRITTEN IN A COUNTRY CHURCHYARD

THE curfew tolls the knell of parting day,
The lowing herd winds slowly o'er the lea,
The ploughman homeward plods his weary way,
And leaves the world to darkness and to me.

Now fades the glimmering landscape on the sight,
And all the air a solemn stillness holds,
Save where the beetle wheels his droning flight,
And drowsy tinklings lull the distant folds.

Save that from yonder ivy-mantled tow'r
The moping owl does to the moon complain
Of such as, wand'ring near her secret bow'r,
Molest her ancient solitary reign.

Beneath those rugged elms, that yew-tree's shade,
Where heaves the turf in many a mould'ring heap,
Each in his narrow cell for ever laid,
The rude Forefathers of the hamlet sleep.

The breezy call of incense-breathing morn,
The swallow twitt'ring from the straw-built shed,
The cock's shrill clarion, or the echoing horn,
No more shall rouse them from their lowly bed.

For them no more the blazing hearth shall burn,
Or busy houswife ply her evening care:
No children run to lisp their sire's return,
Or climb his knees the envied kiss to share.

Oft did the harvest to their sickle yield,
Their furrow oft the stubborn glebe has broke;
How jocund did they drive their team afield!
How bow'd the woods beneath their sturdy stroke!

Let not Ambition mock their useful toil,
Their homely joys, and destiny obscure;
Nor Grandeur hear with a disdainful smile,
The short and simple annals of the Poor.

The boast of heraldry, the pomp of pow'r,
And all that beauty, all that wealth e'er gave,
Await alike th' inevitable hour.
The paths of glory lead but to the grave.

Forgive, ye Proud, th' involuntary fault
If Memory to these no trophies raise,
Where thro' the long-drawn aisle and fretted vault
The pealing anthem swells the note of praise.

Can storied urn or animated bust
Back to its mansion call the fleeting breath ?
Can Honour's voice provoke the silent dust,
Or Flatt'ry soothe the dull cold ear of Death !

Perhaps in this neglected spot is laid
Some heart once pregnant with celestial fire,
Hands that the rod of empire might have sway'd
Or waked to ecstasy the living lyre.

But Knowledge to their eyes her ample page
Rich with the spoils of time did ne'er unroll ;
Chill Penury repress'd their noble rage,
And froze the genial current of the soul.

Full many a gem of purest ray serene,
The dark unfathom'd caves of ocean bear :
Full many a flower is born to blush unseen,
And waste its sweetness on the desert air.

Some village-Hampden, that with dauntless breast
The little tyrant of his fields withstood ;
Some mute inglorious Milton here may rest,
Some Cromwell guiltless of his country's blood.

Th' applause of list'ning senates to command,
The threats of pain and ruin to despise,
To scatter plenty o'er a smiling land,
And read their history in a nation's eyes,

Their lot forbad : nor circumscribed alone
Their growing virtues, but their crimes confined
Forbad to wade through slaughter to a throne,
And shut the gates of mercy on mankind,

The struggling pangs of conscious truth to hide,
To quench the blushes of ingenuous shame,
Or heap the shrine of Luxury and Pride
With incense, kindled at the Muse's flame.

Far from the madding crowd's ignoble strife,
Their sober wishes never learn'd to stray ;
Along the cool sequester'd vale of life
They kept the noiseless tenour of their way.

Yet e'en those bones from insult to protect
Some frail memorial still erected nigh,
With uncouth rhimes and shapeless sculpture deck'd,
Implores the passing tribute of a sigh.

Their name, their years, spelt by th' unletter'd Muse,
The place of fame and elegy supply :
And many a holy text around she strews
That teach the rustic moralist to die.

For who to dumb forgetfulness a prey,
This pleasing anxious being e'er resign'd,
Left the warm precincts of the cheerful day,
Nor cast one longing, ling'ring look behind ?

On some fond breast the parting soul relies,
Some pious drops the closing eye requires ;
E'en from the tomb the voice of Nature cries
E'en in our ashes live their wonted fires.

For thee, who, mindful of th' unhonour'd dead,
Dost in these lines their artless tale relate ;
If chance, by lonely Contemplation led,
Some kindred spirit shall inquire thy fate,

Haply some hoary-headed swain may say,
' Oft have we seen him at the peep of dawn
Brushing with hasty steps the dews away,
To meet the sun upon the upland lawn.

' There at the foot of yonder nodding beech
That wreathes its old fantastic roots so high,
His listless length at noon-tide would he stretch,
And pore upon the brook that babbles by.

' Hard by yon wood, now smiling as in scorn,
Muttering his wayward fancies he would rove ;
Now drooping, woeful wan, like one forlorn,
Or crazed with care, or cross'd in hopeless love.

' One morn I miss'd him on the custom'd hill,
Along the heath, and near his favourite tree ;
Another came ; nor yet beside the rill,
Nor up the lawn, nor at the wood was he.

' The next with dirges due in sad array
Slow thro' the church-way path we saw him borne.
Approach and read (for thou canst read) the lay,
Graved on the stone beneath yon agèd thorn.'

The Epitaph

Herè rests his head upon the lap of Earth
A Youth to Fortune and to Fame unknown :
Fair Science frown'd not on his humble birth,
And Melancholy mark'd him for her own.

Large was his bounty, and his soul sincere,
Heaven did a recompense as largely send :
He gave to Misr'y all he had, a tear :
He gain'd from Heav'n ('twas all he wish'd) a friend.

No farther seek his merits to disclose,
Or draw his frailties from their dread abode,
(There they alike in trembling hope repose,)
The bosom of his Father and his God.

T. GRAY.

ON THE MORNING OF CHRIST'S NATIVITY

This is the month, and this the happy morn
Wherein the Son of heav'n's eternal king
Of wedded Maid, and Virgin Mother born,
Our great redemption from above did bring ;
For so the holy sages once did sing,
That He our deadly forfeit should release,
And with His Father work us a perpetual peace.

That glorious Form, that Light unsufferable,
And that far-beaming blaze of Majesty
Wherewith He wont at Heav'n's high council-table
To sit the midst of Trinal Unity,
He laid aside ; and here with us to be,
Forsook the courts of everlasting day,
And chose with us a darksome house of mortal clay.

Say, heav'nly Muse, shall not thy sacred vein
Afford a present to the Infant God ?
Hast thou no verse, no hymn, or solemn strain,
To welcome Him to this His new abode,
Now while the heav'n by the sun's team untrod,
Hath took no print of the approaching light,
And all the spangled host keep watch in squadrons bright ?

See how from far, upon the eastern road
The star-led wizards haste with odours sweet :
O run, prevent them with thy humble ode,
And lay it lowly at His blessèd feet ;
Have thou the honour first thy Lord to greet,
And join thy voice unto the angel quire,
From out His secret altar touch'd with hallow'd fire.

THE HYMN

It was the winter wild
While the heav'n-born Child
All meanly wrapt in the rude manger lies;
Nature in awe to Him
Had doff'd her gaudy trim,
With her great Master so to sympathise:
It was no season then for her
To wanton with the sun, her lusty paramour.

Only with speeches fair
She woos the gentle air
To hide her guilty front with innocent snow,
And on her naked shame,
Pollute with sinful blame,
The saintly veil of maiden white to throw,
Confounded that her Maker's eyes
Should look so near upon her foul deformities.

But He, her fears to cease,
Sent down the meek-ey'd Peace;
She crown'd with olive green, came softly sliding
Down through the turning sphere,
His ready harbinger,
With turtle wing the amorous clouds dividing;
And waving wide her myrtle wand,
She strikes a universal peace through sea and land.

No war, or battle's sound
Was heard the world around:
The idle spear and shield were high up hung,
The hookèd chariot stood
Unstain'd with hostile blood,
The trumpet spake not to the armèd throng,
And kings sat still with awful eye,
As if they surely knew their sov'reign Lord was by.

But peaceful was the night,
Wherein the Prince of Light

His reign of peace upon the earth began :
The winds, with wonder whist,
Smoothly the waters kist,
Whispering new joys to the mild oceàn,
Who now hath quite forgot to rave,
While birds of calm sit brooding on the charmèd wave.

The stars with deep amaze,
Stand fix'd in steadfast gaze,
Bending one way their precious influence,
And will not take their flight,
For all the morning light,
Or Lucifer that often warn'd them thence ;
But in their glimmering orbs did glow,
Until their Lord Himself bespake, and bid them go.

And though the shady gloom
Had given day her room,
The sun himself withheld his wonted speed,
And hid his head for shame,
As his inferior flame
The new-enlighten'd world no more should need ;
He saw a greater Sun appear
Than his bright throne, or burning axletree, could bear.

The shepherds on the lawn,
Or ere the point of dawn,
Sate simply chatting in a rustic row ;
Full little thought they then
That the mighty Pan
Was kindly come to live with them below ;
Perhaps their loves, or else their sheep,
Was all that did their silly thoughts so busy keep.

When such music sweet
Their hearts and ears did greet,
As never was by mortal finger strook,
Divinely-warbled voice
Answering the stringèd noise,
As all their souls in blissful rapture took :
The air, such pleasure loth to lose,
With thousand echoes still prolongs each heavenly close.

X

Nature that heard such sound,
Beneath the hollow round
Of Cynthia's seat, the airy region thrilling,
Now was almost won
To think her part was done,
And that her reign had here its last fulfilling;
She knew such harmony alone
Could hold all heav'n and earth in happier union.

At last surrounds their sight
A globe of circular light,
That with long beams the shamefac'd night array'd;
The helmèd Cherubim,
And sworded Seraphim,
Are seen in glittering ranks with wings display'd,
Harping in loud and solemn quire,
With unexpressive notes to Heaven's new-born Heir.

Such music (as 'tis said)
Before was never made,
But when of old the Sons of Morning sung,
While the Creator great
His constellations set,
And the well-balanc'd world on hinges hung,
And cast the dark foundations deep,
And bid the welt'ring waves their oozy channel keep.

Ring out, ye crystal spheres,
Once bless our human ears,
If ye have power to touch our senses so;
And let your silver chime
Move in melodious time,
And let the bass of Heav'n's deep organ blow;
And with your ninefold harmony
Make up full consort to th' angelic symphony.

For if such holy song
Inwrap our fancy long,
Time will run back, and fetch the age of gold,
And speckled Vanity
Will sicken soon and die,
And leprous Sin will melt from earthly mould

And Hell itself will pass away,
And leave her dolorous mansions to the peering day.

Yea, Truth and Justice then
Will down return to men,
Orb'd in a rainbow ; and, like glories wearing,
Mercy will set between,
Throned in celestial sheen,
With radiant feet the tissued clouds down steering :
And Heav'n, as at some festival,
Will open wide the gates of her high palace hall.

But wisest Fate says, No,
This must not yet be so,
The Babe yet lies in smiling infancy,
That on the bitter cross
Must redeem our loss ;
So both himself and us to glorify ;
Yet first to those ychain'd in sleep,
The wakeful trump of doom must thunder through the deep,

With such a horrid clang
As on mount Sinai rang,
While the red fire and smouldering clouds outbrake :
The aged Earth aghast,
With terror of that blast,
Shall from the surface to the centre shake ;
When at the world's last session,
The dreadful Judge in middle air shall spread his throne.

And then at last our bliss
Full and perfect is,
But now begins ; for from this happy day
The old Dragon under ground
In straiter limits bound,
Not half so far casts his usurpèd sway,
And wroth to see his kingdom fail,
Swinges the scaly horror of his folded tail.

The oracles are dumb,
No voice or hideous hum

Runs thro' the archèd roof in words deceiving.
Apollo from his shrine
Can no more divine,
With hollow shriek the steep of Delphos leaving.

No nightly trance or breathèd spell
Inspires the pale-ey'd priest from the prophetic cell.

The lonely mountains o'er,
And the resounding shore,
A voice of weeping heard, and loud lament;
From haunted spring and dale
Edg'd with poplar pale,
The parting Genius is with sighing sent;
With flow'r-inwoven tresses torn
The Nymphs in twilight shade of tangled thickets mourn.

In consecrated earth,
And, on the holy hearth,
The Lars, and Lemures moan with midnight plaint;
In urns, and altars round,
A drear and dying sound
Affrights the Flamens at their service quaint;
And the chill marble seems to sweat,
While each peculiar Power forgoes his wonted seat.

Peor and Baälim
Forsake their temples dim,
With that twice-batter'd god of Palestine;
And moonèd Ashtaroth,
Heaven's queen and mother both,
Now sits not girt with tapers' holy shine;
The Lybic Hammon shrinks his horn.
In vain the Tyrian maids their wounded Thammuz mourn.

And sullen Moloch fled,
Hath left in shadows dread
His burning idol all of blackest hue;
In vain with cymbals' ring
They call the grisly king,
In dismal dance about the furnace blue:
The brutish gods of Nile as fast,
Isis and Orus, and the dog Anubis haste.

Nor is Osiris seen
In Memphian grove or green,

Trampling the unshow'r'd grass with lowings loud:
Nor can he be at rest
Within his sacred chest,
Nought but profoundest hell can be his shroud;

In vain with timbrell'd anthems dark
The sable-stolèd sorcerers bear his worship'd ark.

He feels from Juda's land
The dreaded infant's hand,
The rays of Bethlehem blind his dusky eyn;
Not all the gods beside,
Longer dare abide,
Not Typhon huge ending in snaky twine:
Our Babe, to show his Godhead true,
Can in his swaddling bands control the damnèd crew.

So, when the sun in bed,
Curtain'd with cloudy red,
Pillows his chin upon an orient wave,
The flocking shadows pale
Troop to th' infernal jail,
Each fetter'd ghost slips to his several grave;
And the yellow-skirted Fayes
Fly after the night-steeds, leaving their moon-loved maze.

But see the Virgin blest
Hath laid her Babe to rest;
Time is, our tedious song should here have ending;
Heav'n's youngest teemèd star
Hath fix'd her polish'd car,
Her sleeping Lord with handmaid lamp attending;
And all about the courtly stable
Bright-harness'd Angels sit in order serviceable.

J. MILTON.

WINTER

In a drear-nighted December,
Too happy, happy Tree,
Thy branches ne'er remember
Their green felicity:
The north cannot undo them,
With a sleety whistle through them;
Nor frozen thawings glue them
From budding at the prime.

In a drear-nighted December,
Too happy, happy Brook,
Thy bubblings ne'er remember
Apollo's summer look;
But with a sweet forgetting,
They stay their crystal fretting,
Never, never petting
About the frozen time.

Ah, would 'twere so with many
A gentle girl and boy!
But were there ever any
Writh'd not at passèd joy?
To know the change and feel it,
When there is none to heal it,
Nor numbèd sense to steal it,
Was never said in rhyme.

J. KEATS.

CHRISTABEL

'TIS the middle of night by the castle clock,
And the owls have awakened the crowing cock!
Tu—whit!——Tu—whoo!
And hark, again! the crowing cock,
How drowsily it crew.

Sir Leoline, the Baron rich,
Hath a toothless mastiff bitch
From her kennel beneath the rock
Maketh answer to the clock,
Four for the quarters, and twelve for the hour;
Ever and aye, by shine and shower,
Sixteen short howls, not over loud:
Some say, she sees my lady's shroud.

Is the night chilly and dark?
The night is chilly, but not dark·

The thin gray cloud is spread on high,
It covers but not hides the sky.
The moon is behind, and at the full;
And yet she looks both small and dull.
The night is chill, the cloud is gray:
'Tis a month before the month of May,
And the Spring comes slowly up this way.

The lovely lady, Christabel,
Whom her father loves so well,
What makes her in the wood so late,
A furlong from the castle gate?
She had dreams all yesternight
Of her own betrothed knight;
And she in the midnight wood will pray
For the weal of her lover that's far away.

She stole along, she nothing spoke,
The sighs she heaved were soft and low,
And naught was green upon the oak,
But moss and rarest misletoe;
She kneels beneath the huge oak tree,
And in silence prayeth she.

The lady sprang up suddenly,
The lovely lady, Christabel!
It moaned as near, as near can be,
But what it is, she cannot tell.—
On the other side it seems to be,
Of the huge, broad-breasted, old oak tree.

The night is chill; the forest bare;
Is it the wind that moaneth bleak?
There is not wind enough in the air
To move away the ringlet curl
From the lovely lady's cheek—
There is not wind enough to twirl
The one red leaf, the last of its clan,
That dances as often as dance it can,
Hanging so light, and hanging so high,
On the topmost twig that looks up to the sky.

Hush, beating heart of Christabel !
Jesu, Maria, shield her well !
She folded her arms beneath her cloak,
And stole to the other side of the oak.
  What sees she there ?

There she sees a damsel bright,
Drest in a silken robe of white,
That shadowy in the moonlight shone :
The neck that made that white robe wan,
Her stately neck, and arms were bare :
Her blue-veined feet unsandaled were ;
And wildly glittered here and there
The gems entangled in her hair.
I guess, 'twas frightful there to see
A lady so richly clad as she—
Beautiful exceedingly !

Mary mother, save me now !
(Said Christabel), And who art thou ?

The lady strange made answer meet,
And her voice was faint and sweet :—
Have pity on my sore distress,
I scarce can speak for weariness.
Stretch forth thy hand, and have no fear,
Said Christabel, How camest thou here ?
And the lady, whose voice was faint and sweet
Did thus pursue her answer meet :—

My sire is of a noble line,
And my name is Geraldine :
Five warriors seized me yestermorn,
Me, even me, a maid forlorn :
They choked my cries with force and fright,
And tied me on a palfrey white.
The palfrey was as fleet as wind,
And they rode furiously behind.
They spurred amain, their steeds were white ;
And once we crossed the shade of night.

As sure as Heaven shall rescue me,
I have no thought what men they be;
Nor do I know how long it is
(For I have lain entranced I wis)

Since one, the tallest of the five,
Took me from the palfrey's back,
A weary woman, scarce alive.
Some muttered words his comrades spoke:
He placed me underneath this oak,

He swore they would return with haste
Whither they went I cannot tell—
I thought I heard, some minutes past,
Sounds as of a castle bell.
Stretch forth thy hand (thus ended she),
And help a wretched maid to flee.

Then Christabel stretched forth her hand
And comforted fair Geraldine :
O well bright dame may you command
The service of Sir Leoline ;
And gladly our stout chivalry
Will he send forth and friends withal
To guide and guard you safe and free
Home to your noble father's hall.
She rose : and forth with steps they passed
That strove to be, and were not, fast.
Her gracious stars the lady blest,
And thus spake on sweet Christabel ;
All our household are at rest,
The hall as silent as the cell,
Sir Leoline is weak in health
And may not well awakened be,
But we will move as if in stealth ;
And I beseech your courtesy
This night, to share your couch with me.

They crossed the moat, and Christabel
Took the key that fitted well ;
A little door she opened straight,
All in the middle of the gate ;
The gate that was ironed within and without,
Where an army in battle-array had marched out.
The lady sank, belike through pain,
And Christabel with might and main
Lifted her up, a weary weight,
Over the threshold of the gate :
Then the lady rose again,
And moved, as she were not in pain.

So free from danger, free from fear,
They crossed the court: right glad they were.
And Christabel devoutly cried
To the lady by her side,
Praise we the Virgin all divine
Who hath rescued thee from thy distress!
Alas, alas! said Geraldine,
I cannot speak for weariness.
So free from danger, free from fear,
They crossed the court: right glad they were.

Outside her kennel, the mastiff old
Lay fast asleep, in moonshine cold.
The mastiff old did not awake,
Yet she an angry moan did make!
And what can ail the mastiff bitch?
Never till now she uttered yell
Beneath the eye of Christabel.
Perhaps it is the owlet's scritch:
For what can ail the mastiff bitch?

They passed the hall, that echoes still,
Pass as lightly as you will!
The brands were flat, the brands were dying,
Amid their own white ashes lying;
But when the lady passed, there came
A tongue of light, a fit of flame;
And Christabel saw the lady's eye,
And nothing else saw she thereby,
Save the boss of the shield of Sir Leoline tall
Which hung in a murky old niche in the wall.
O softly tread, said Christabel,
My father seldom sleepeth well.

Sweet Christabel her feet doth bare,
And jealous of the listening air
They steal their way from stair to stair.
Now in glimmer, and now in gloom,
And now they pass the Baron's room.

As still as death with stifled breath !
And now have reached her chamber door ;
And now doth Geraldine press down
The rushes of the chamber floor.

The moon shines dim in the open air,
And not a moonbeam enters here.
But they without its light can see
The chamber carved so curiously,
Carved with figures strange and sweet,
All made out of the carver's brain,
For a lady's chamber meet :
The lamp with twofold silver chain
Is fastened to an angel's feet.

The silver lamp burns dead and dim ;
But Christabel the lamp will trim.
She trimm'd the lamp, and made it bright,
And left it swinging to and fro,
While Geraldine, in wretched plight,
Sank down upon the floor below.

' O weary lady, Geraldine,
I pray you, drink this cordial wine !
It is a wine of virtuous powers ;
My mother made it of wild flowers.'

' And will your mother pity me,
Who am a maiden most forlorn ? '
Christabel answered—' Woe is me !
She died the hour that I was born.
I have heard the grey-hair'd friar tell,
How on her death-bed she did say,
That she should hear the castle-bell
Strike twelve upon my wedding-day.
O mother dear ! that thou wert here ! '
' I would,' said Geraldine, ' she were ! '

But soon with altered voice, said she—
' Off, wandering mother ! Peak and pine !
I have power to bid thee flee.'
Alas ! what ails poor Geraldine ?

Why stares she with unsettled eye ?
Can she the bodiless dead espy ?
And why with hollow voice cries she,
' Off, woman, off! this hour is mine—
Though thou her guardian spirit be,
Off, woman, off! 'tis given to me.'

Then Christabel knelt by the lady's side,
And raised to heaven her eyes so blue—
' Alas ! ' said she, ' this ghastly ride—
Dear lady ! it hath 'wilder'd you ! '
The lady wiped her moist cold brow,
And faintly said, ' 'Tis over now ! '

Again the wild-flower wine she drank :
Her fair large eyes 'gan glitter bright,
And from the floor whereon she sank,
The lofty lady stood upright :
She was most beautiful to see,
Like a lady of a far countrèe.

And thus the lofty lady spake—
' All they who live in the upper sky,
Do love you, holy Christabel !
And you love them, and for their sake
And for the good which me befell,
Even I in my degree will try,
Fair maiden, to requite you well.
But now unrobe yourself ; for I
Must pray, ere yet in bed I lie.'
Quoth Christabel, ' So let it be ! '
And as the lady bade, did she.
Her gentle limbs did she undress,
And lay down in her loveliness.

But through her brain of weal and woe
So many thoughts moved to and fro,
That vain it were her lids to close ;
So half-way from the bed she rose,
And on her elbow did recline
To look at the lady Geraldine.

Beneath the lamp the lady bow'd,
And slowly roll'd her eyes around ;
Then drawing in her breath aloud
Like one that shudder'd, she unbound
The cincture from beneath her breast :
Her silken robe, and inner vest,
Dropt to her feet, and full in view,
Behold ! her bosom and half her side——
A sight to dream of, not to tell !
O shield her ! shield sweet Christabel !

Yet Geraldine nor speaks nor stirs ;
Ah ! what a stricken look was hers !
Deep from within she seems half-way
To lift some weight with sick assay,
And eyes the maid and seeks delay ;
Then suddenly, as one defied,
Collects herself in scorn and pride,
And lay down by the maiden's side !—
And in her arms the maid she took,
        Ah well-a-day !
And with low voice and doleful look
These words did say :
' In the touch of this bosom there worketh a spell,
Which is lord of thy utterance, Christabel !
Thou knowest to-night, and wilt know to-morrow,
This mark of my shame, this seal of my sorrow ;
        But vainly thou warrest,
          For this is alone in
        Thy power to declare,
          That in the dim forest
        Thou heard'st a low moaning,
And found'st a bright lady, surpassingly fair ;
And didst bring her home with thee in love and in
        charity,
To shield her and shelter her from the damp air.'

S. T. COLERIDGE.

SO HALF-WAY FROM THE BED SHE ROSE,
AND ON HER ELBOW DID RECLINE
TO LOOK AT THE LADY GERALDINE.

Y

YARROW UNVISITED

1803

FROM Stirling Castle we had seen
The mazy Forth unravelled;
Had trod the banks of Clyde, and Tay,
And with the Tweed had travell'd;
And when we came to Clovenford,
Then said my 'winsome Marrow,'
' Whate'er betide, we'll turn aside,
And see the Braes of Yarrow.'

' Let Yarrow folk, frae Selkirk town,
Who have been buying, selling,
Go back to Yarrow, 'tis their own;
Each maiden to her dwelling!
On Yarrow's banks let herons feed,
Hares couch, and rabbits burrow!
But we will downward with the Tweed,
Nor turn aside to Yarrow.

' There's Gala Water, Leader Haughs,
Both lying right before us;
And Dryburgh, where with chiming Tweed
The lintwhites sing in chorus;
There's pleasant Teviot-dale, a land
Made blythe with plough and harrow:
Why throw away a needful day
To go in search of Yarrow?

' What's Yarrow but a river bare,
That glides the dark hills under?
There are a thousand such elsewhere
As worthy of your wonder.'
—Strange words they seemed of slight and scorn;
My true-love sigh'd for sorrow,
And looked me in the face, to think
I thus could speak of Yarrow!

'Oh! green,' said I, 'are Yarrow's holms,
And sweet is Yarrow flowing!
Fair hangs the apple frae the rock,
But we will leave it growing.
O'er hilly path, and open strath,
We'll wander Scotland thorough;
But, though so near, we will not turn
Into the dale of Yarrow.

'Let beeves and home-bred kine partake
The sweets of Burn-Mill meadow;
The swan on still Saint Mary's Lake
Float double, swan and shadow!
We will not see them; will not go,
To-day, nor yet to-morrow;
Enough if in our hearts we know
There's such a place as Yarrow.

'Be Yarrow stream unseen, unknown!
It must, or we shall rue it:
We have a vision of our own;
Ah! why should we undo it?
The treasured dreams of times long past,
We'll keep them, winsome Marrow!
For when we're there, although 'tis fair,
'Twill be another Yarrow!

'If care with freezing years should come,
And wandering seem but folly,—
Should we be loth to stir from home,
And yet be melancholy;
Should life be dull, and spirits low,
'Twill soothe us in our sorrow,
That earth has something yet to show,
The bonny Holms of Yarrow!'

W. WORDSWORTH.

YARROW VISITED

September 1814

AND is this—Yarrow?—This the Stream
Of which my fancy cherished,
So faithfully, a waking dream,
An image that hath perished?
O that some minstrel's harp were near,
To utter notes of gladness,
And chase this silence from the air,
That fills my heart with sadness!

Yet why?—a silvery current flows
With uncontroll'd meanderings;
Nor have these eyes by greener hills
Been soothed, in all my wanderings.
And, through her depths, Saint Mary's Lake
Is visibly delighted;
For not a feature of those hills
Is in the mirror slighted.

A blue sky bends o'er Yarrow Vale,
Save where that pearly whiteness
Is round the rising sun diffused,
A tender hazy brightness;
Mild dawn of promise! that excludes
All profitless dejection;
Though not unwilling here to admit
A pensive recollection.

Where was it that the famous Flower
Of Yarrow Vale lay bleeding?
His bed perchance was yon smooth mound
On which the herd is feeding:
And haply from this crystal pool,
Now peaceful as the morning,
The Water-wraith ascended thrice—
And gave his doleful warning.

Delicious is the Lay that sings
The haunts of happy lovers,
The path that leads them to the grove,
The leafy grove that covers:
And pity sanctifies the verse
That paints, by strength of sorrow,
The unconquerable strength of love;
Bear witness, rueful Yarrow!

But thou that didst appear so fair
To fond imagination,
Dost rival in the light of day
Her delicate creation:
Meek loveliness is round thee spread,
A softness still and holy;
The grace of forest charms decayed,
And pastoral melancholy.

That region left, the vale unfolds
Rich groves of lofty stature,
With Yarrow winding through the pomp
Of cultivated Nature;
And rising from those lofty groves,
Behold a ruin hoary!
The shattered front of Newark's Towers,
Renowned in Border story.

Fair scenes for childhood's opening bloom,
For sportive youth to stray in,
For manhood to enjoy his strength;
And age to wear away in!
Yon cottage seems a bower of bliss,
A covert for protection
Of studious ease and generous cares,
And every chaste affection!

How sweet on this autumnal day
The wild-wood fruits to gather,
And on my true-love's forehead plant
A crest of blooming heather!

And what if I enwreathed my own ?
'Twere no offence to reason ;
The sober hills thus deck their brows
To meet the wintry season.

I see—but not by sight alone,
Loved Yarrow, have I won thee;
A ray of Fancy still survives—
Her sunshine plays upon thee !
Thy ever-youthful waters keep
A course of lively pleasure ;
And gladsome notes my lips can breathe,
Accordant to the measure.

The vapours linger round the heights,
They melt, and soon must vanish ;
One hour is theirs, nor more is mine—
Sad thought, which I would banish,
But that I know, where'er I go,
Thy genuine image, Yarrow !
Will dwell with me—to heighten joy
And cheer my mind in sorrow.

W. WORDSWORTH.

SIR HUGH; OR, THE JEW'S DAUGHTER

YESTERDAY was brave Hallowday,
And, above all days of the year,
The schoolboys all got leave to play,
And little Sir Hugh was there.

He kicked the ball with his foot,
And kepped it with his knee,
And even in at the Jew's window,
He gart the bonnie ba' flee.

Out then came the Jew's daughter—
    ' Will ye come in and dine ? '
' I winna come in and I canna come in,
    Till I get that ball of mine.

' Throw down that ball to me, maiden,
    Throw down the ball to me.'
' I winna throw down your ball, Sir Hugh,
    Till ye come up to me.'

She pu'd the apple frae the tree,
    It was baith red and green,
She gave it unto little Sir Hugh,
    With that his heart did win.

She wiled him into ae chamber,
    She wiled him into twa,
She wiled him into the third chamber,
    And that was warst o't a'.

She took out a little penknife,
    Hung low down by her gair,
She twined this young thing o' his life,
    And a word he ne'er spak mair.

And first came out the thick, thick blood,
    And syne came out the thin,
And syne came out the bonnie heart's blood
    There was nae mair within.

She laid him on a dressing-table,
    She dress'd him like a swine,
Says, ' Lie ye there, my bonnie Sir Hugh,
    Wi' ye're apples red and green.'

She put him in a case of lead,
    Says, ' Lie ye there and sleep ; '
She threw him into the deep draw-well
    Was fifty fathom deep.

A schoolboy walking in the garden,
　Did grievously hear him moan,
He ran away to the deep draw-well
　And on his knee fell down.

Says 'Bonnie Sir Hugh, and pretty Sir Hugh,
    I pray you speak to me;
If you speak to any body in this world,
    I pray you speak to me.'

When bells were rung and mass was sung,
    And every body went hame,
Then every lady had her son,
    But Lady Helen had nane.

She rolled her mantle her about,
    And sore, sore did she weep;
She ran away to the Jew's castle
    When all were fast asleep.

She cries, 'Bonnie Sir Hugh, O pretty Sir Hugh,
    I pray you speak to me;
If you speak to any body in this world,
    I pray you speak to me.'

' Lady Helen, if ye want your son,
    I'll tell ye where to seek;
Lady Helen, if ye want your son,
    He's in the well sae deep.'

She ran away to the deep draw-well,
    And she fell down on her knee;
Saying, 'Bonnie Sir Hugh, O pretty Sir Hugh,
    I pray ye speak to me,
If ye speak to any body in the world,
    I pray ye speak to me.'

' Oh ! the lead it is wondrous heavy, mother,
    The well it is wondrous deep,
The little penknife sticks in my throat,
    And I downa to ye speak.

'But lift me out o' this deep draw-well,
 And bury me in yon churchyard;
Put a Bible at my head,' he says,
 'And a testament at my feet,
And pen and ink at every side,
 And I'll lie still and sleep.

'And go to the back of Maitland town,
 Bring me my winding-sheet;
For it's at the back of Maitland town
 That you and I sall meet.'

O the broom, the bonny, bonny broom
 The broom that makes full sore;
A woman's mercy is very little,
 But a man's mercy is more.

ANONYMOUS.

A LYKE-WAKE DIRGE

THIS ae nighte, this ae nighte,
 Every nighte and alle,
Fire, and sleet, and candle lighte,
 And Christe receive thye saule.

When thou from hence away art paste,
 Every nighte and alle,
To Whinny-muir thou comest at laste,
 And Christe receive thye saule.

If ever thou gavest hosen and shoon,
 Every nighte and alle,
Sit thee down and put them on,
 And Christe receive thye saule.

If hosen and shoon thou ne'er gavest nane,
 Every nighte and alle,
The whinnes sall pricke thee to the bare bane;
 And Christe receive thye saule.

From Whinny-muir when thou mayst passe,
  Every nighte and alle,
To Brigg o' Dread thou comest at laste,
  And Christe receive thye saule.

    .   .   .   .   .   .

From Brigg o' Dread when thou mayst passe,
  Every nighte and alle,
To Purgatory fire thou comest at last,
  And Christe receive thye saule.

If ever thou gavest meat or drink,
  Every nighte and alle,
The fire sall never make thee shrinke,
  And Christe receive thye saule.

If meate or drinke thou never gavest nane,
  Every nighte and alle,
The fire will burn thee to the bare bane;
  And Christe receive thye saule.

This ae nighte, this ae nighte,
  Every nighte and alle,
Fire, and sleet, and candle lighte,
  And Christe receive thye saule.

THE RED FISHERMAN; OR, THE DEVIL'S DECOY

'Oh flesh, flesh, how art thou fishified.'—*Romeo and Juliet.*

THE Abbot arose, and closed his book,
  And donned his sandal shoon,
And wandered forth, alone, to look
  Upon the summer moon:
A starlight sky was o'er his head,
  A quiet breeze around;
And the flowers a thrilling fragrance shed,
  And the waves a soothing sound:

It was not an hour, nor a scene, for aught
  But love and calm delight;
Yet the holy man had a cloud of thought
  On his wrinkled brow that night.

He gazed on the river that gurgled by,
  But he thought not of the reeds;
He clasped his gilded rosary,
  But he did not tell the beads;
If he looked to the heaven, 'twas not to invoke
  The Spirit that dwelleth there;
If he opened his lips, the words they spoke
  Had never the tone of prayer.
A pious priest might the Abbot seem,
  He had swayed the crozier well;
But what was the theme of the Abbot's dream,
  The Abbot were loath to tell.

Companionless, for a mile or more
He traced the windings of the shore
Oh, beauteous is that river still,
As it winds by many a sloping hill,
And many a dim o'erarching grove,
And many a flat and sunny cove,
And terraced lawns, whose bright arcades
The honeysuckle sweetly shades,
And rocks, whose very crags seem bowers,
So gay they are with grass and flowers!
But the Abbot was thinking of scenery
  About as much, in sooth,
As a lover thinks of constancy,
  Or an advocate of truth.
He did not mark how the skies in wrath
  Grew dark above his head;
He did not mark how the mossy path
  Grew damp beneath his tread;
And nearer he came, and still more near,
  To a pool, in whose recess
The water had slept for many a year
  Unchanged and motionless;

From the river-stream it spread away
  The space of half a rood;
The surface had the hue of clay
  And the scent of human blood;
The trees and the herbs that round it grew
  Were venomous and foul,
And the birds that through the bushes flew
  Were the vulture and the owl;
The water was as dark and rank
  As ever a company pumped,
And the perch, that was netted and laid on the bank,
  Grew rotten while it jumped;
And bold was he who thither came
  At midnight, man or boy,
For the place was cursed with an evil name,
  And that name was ' The Devil's Decoy!'

The Abbot was weary as abbot could be,
And he sat down to rest on the stump of a tree:
When suddenly rose a dismal tone,—
Was it a song, or was it a moan?—
     ' O ho! O ho!
     Above,—below,—
Lightly and brightly they glide and go!
The hungry and keen on the top are leaping,
The lazy and fat in the depths are sleeping;
Fishing is fine when the pool is muddy,
Broiling is rich when the coals are ruddy! '
In a monstrous fright, by the murky light,
He looked to the left and he looked to the right,
And what was the vision close before him,
That flung such a sudden stupor o'er him?
'Twas a sight to make the hair uprise,
    And the life-blood colder run:
The startled Priest struck both his thighs,
    And the abbey clock struck one!

All alone, by the side of the pool,
A tall man sat on a three-legged stool,
Kicking his heels on the dewy sod,
And putting in order his reel and rod;

Red were the rags his shoulders wore,
And a high red cap on his head he bore ;
His arms and his legs were long and bare ;
And two or three locks of long red hair
Were tossing about his scraggy neck,
Like a tattered flag o'er a splitting wreck.
It might be time, or it might be trouble,
Had bent that stout back nearly double,
Sunk in their deep and hollow sockets
That blazing couple of Congreve rockets,
And shrunk and shrivelled that tawny skin
Till it hardly covered the bones within.
The line the Abbot saw him throw
Had been fashioned and formed long ages ago.
And the hands that worked his foreign vest
Long ages ago had gone to their rest :
You would have sworn, as you looked on them,
He had fished in the flood with Ham and Shem !

There was turning of keys, and creaking of locks,
As he took forth a bait from his iron box.
Minnow or gentle, worm or fly,—
It seemed not such to the Abbot's eye ;
Gaily it glittered with jewel and gem,
And its shape was the shape of a diadem.
It was fastened a gleaming hook about
By a chain within and a chain without ;
The Fisherman gave it a kick and a spin,
And the water fizzed as it tumbled in !

From the bowels of the earth
Strange and varied sounds had birth :
Now the battle's bursting peal,
Neigh of steed, and clang of steel ;
Now an old man's hollow groan
Echoed from the dungeon stone ;
Now the weak and wailing cry
Of a stripling's agony !—
Cold by this was the midnight air ;

But the Abbot's blood ran colder,
When he saw a gasping Knight lie there,
With a gash beneath his clotted hair,
 And a hump upon his shoulder.
 And the loyal churchman strove in vain

To mutter a Pater Noster;
For he who writhed in mortal pain
Was camped that night on Bosworth plain—
 The cruel Duke of Gloster!

There was turning of keys, and creaking of locks
As he took forth a bait from his iron box.
It was a haunch of princely size,
Filling with fragrance earth and skies.
The corpulent Abbot knew full well
The swelling form, and the steaming smell:

Never a monk that wore a hood
Could better have guessed the very wood
Where the noble hart had stood at bay,
Weary and wounded, at close of day.

Sounded then the noisy glee
Of a revelling company,—
Sprightly story, wicked jest,
Rated servant, greeted guest,
Flow of wine and flight of cork,
Stroke of knife and thrust of fork:
But, where'er the board was spread,
Grace, I ween, was never said!—
Pulling and tugging the Fisherman sat;
　　And the Priest was ready to vomit,
When he hauled out a gentleman, fine and fat,
With a belly as big as a brimming vat,
　　And a nose as red as a comet.
'A capital stew,' the Fisherman said,
　　'With cinnamon and sherry!'
And the Abbot turned away his head,
For his brother was lying before him dead—
　　The Mayor of St. Edmund's Bury!

There was turning of keys, and creaking of locks,
As he took forth a bait from his iron box.
It was a bundle of beautiful things,—
A peacock's tail, and a butterfly's wings,
A scarlet slipper, an auburn curl,
A mantle of silk, and a bracelet of pearl,
And a packet of letters, from whose sweet fold
Such a stream of delicate odours rolled,
That the Abbot fell on his face, and fainted,
And deemed his spirit was half-way sainted.

Sounds seemed dropping from the skies,
Stifled whispers, smothered sighs,
And the breath of vernal gales,
And the voice of nightingales:
But the nightingales were mute,
Envious, when an unseen lute

Shaped the music of its chords
Into passion's thrilling words:
'Smile, Lady, smile! I will not set
Upon my brow the coronet,

Till thou wilt gather roses white
To wear around its gems of light.
Smile, Lady, smile !—I will not see
Rivers and Hastings bend the knee,
Till those bewitching lips of thine
Will bid me rise in bliss from mine.
Smile, Lady, smile !—for who would win
A loveless throne through guilt and sin ?
Or who would reign o'er vale and hill,
If woman's heart were rebel still ? '

One jerk, and there a lady lay,
  A lady wondrous fair ;
But the rose of her lip had faded away,
And her cheek was as white and as cold as clay,
  And torn was her raven hair.
' Ah, ha ! ' said the Fisher, in merry guise,
  ' Her gallant was hooked before ; '
And the Abbot heaved some piteous sighs,
For oft he had blessed those deep-blue eyes,
  The eyes of Mistress Shore !

There was turning of keys, and creaking of locks,
As he took forth a bait from his iron box.
Many the cunning sportsman tried,
Many he flung with a frown aside ;
A minstrel's harp, and a miser's chest,
A hermit's cowl, and a baron's crest,
Jewels of lustre, robes of price,
Tomes of heresy, loaded dice,
And golden cups of the brightest wine
That ever was pressed from the Burgundy vine.
There was a perfume of sulphur and nitre,
As he came at last to a bishop's mitre !

From top to toe the Abbot shook,
As the Fisherman armed his golden hook,
And awfully were his features wrought
By some dark dream or wakened thought.
Look how the fearful felon gazes
On the scaffold his country's vengeance raises,

When the lips are cracked and the jaws are dry
With the thirst which only in death shall die:
Mark the mariner's frenzied frown
As the swirling wherry settles down,
When peril has numbed the sense and will,
Though the hand and the foot may struggle still:

Wilder far was the Abbot's glance,
Deeper far was the Abbot's trance:
Fixed as a monument, still as air,
He bent no knee, and he breathed no prayer
But he signed—he knew not why or how,—
The sign of the Cross on his clammy brow.

There was turning of keys, and creaking of locks,
As he stalked away with his iron box.
  ' O ho ! O ho !
  The cock doth crow;
It is time for the Fisher to rise and go.
Fair luck to the Abbot, fair luck to the shrine !
He hath gnawed in twain my choicest line;
Let him swim to the north, let him swim to the south,
The Abbot will carry my hook in his mouth ! '

The Abbot had preached for many years
  With as clear articulation
As ever was heard in the House of Peers
  Against Emancipation;
His words had made battalions quake,
  Had roused the zeal of martyrs,
Had kept the Court an hour awake,
  And the King himself three-quarters:
But ever since that hour, 'tis said,
  He stammered and he stuttered,
As if an axe went through his head
  With every word he uttered.
He stuttered o'er blessing, he stuttered o'er ban,
  He stuttered drunk or dry;
And none but he and the Fisherman
  Could tell the reason why !

         W. M. PRAED.

BOADICEA

AN ODE

WHEN the British warrior-queen,
  Bleeding from the Roman rods,
Sought, with an indignant mien,
  Counsel of her country's gods,

Sage beneath a spreading oak
  Sat the Druid, hoary chief,
Ev'ry burning word he spoke,
  Full of rage and full of grief.

' Princess ! if our aged eyes
  Weep upon thy matchless wrongs,
'Tis because resentment ties
  All the terrors of our tongues.

' Rome shall perish—write that word
  In the blood that she has spilt ;
Perish, hopeless and abhorr'd,
  Deep in ruin as in guilt.

' Rome, for empire far renown'd,
  Tramples on a thousand states ;
Soon her pride shall kiss the ground—
  Hark ! the Gaul is at her gates.

' Other Romans shall arise,
  Heedless of a soldier's name ;
Sounds, not arms, shall win the prize,
  Harmony the path to fame.

' Then the progeny that springs
  From the forests of our land,
Arm'd with thunder, clad with wings,
  Shall a wider world command.

'Regions Cæsar never knew
  Thy posterity shall sway,
Where his eagles never flew,
  None invincible as they.'

Such the bard's prophetic words,
  Pregnant with celestial fire,
Bending as he swept the chords
  Of his sweet but awful lyre.

She, with all a monarch's pride,
  Felt them in her bosom glow,
Rush'd to battle, fought, and died;
  Dying, hurl'd them at the foe.

Ruffians, pitiless as proud,
 Heav'n awards the vengeance due ;
Empire is on us bestow'd,
 Shame and ruin wait for you.

W. COWPER.

ON THE DEPARTURE OF SIR WALTER SCOTT FROM ABBOTSFORD FOR NAPLES [1831]

A TROUBLE, not of clouds, or weeping rain,
Nor of the setting sun's pathetic light
Engendered, hangs o'er Eildon's triple height ;
Spirits of Power, assembled there, complain
For kindred Power departing from their sight ;
While Tweed, best pleased in chanting a blithe strain,
Saddens his voice again, and yet again.
Lift up your hearts, ye Mourners ! for the might
Of the whole world's good wishes with him goes ;
Blessings and prayers in nobler retinue
Than sceptred king or laurelled conqueror knows,
Follow this wondrous Potentate.   Be true,
Ye winds of ocean, and the midland sea,
Wafting your Charge to soft Parthenope !

W. WORDSWORTH.

INDEX OF FIRST LINES